YOU'RE NOT EDITH

YOU'RE NOT EDITH

by Allison Gruber

AUTOBIOGRAPHICAL ESSAYS

GEORGE BRAZILLER / NEW YORK

For my friend and first mentor, Dr. Lynn Loewen

The author wishes to thank the editors at *Windy City Queer*, where an earlier version of "The Mountain" first appeared; and *The Literary Review*, where "Music in the Head" first appeared.

George Braziller, Inc.
277 Broadway, Suite 708
New York, NY 10007

Library of Congress Cataloging-in-Publication Data
Gruber, Allison.
[Essays. Selections]
You're not Edith : autobiographical essays / by Allison Gruber.—First edition.
    pages cm
ISBN 978-0-8076-0005-4
1. Gruber, Allison. 2. Authors, American—21st century—Biography. I. Title.
PS3607.R6788Z46 2015
818'.603—dc23
[B]
                    2014031174

First edition
Designed by Rita Lascaro
Cover photograph: Copyright © www.bertbeckers.be
Printed in the United States of America

CONTENTS

YOU'RE NOT EDITH

The Mountain

Standing in the ape house at Lincoln Park Zoo, I watch two chimpanzees groom one another. The larger chimp preens the smaller. The crowd coos.

"Cutest thing ever," a woman says.

At no other exhibit in the zoo is one more likely to hear "cute" and "I feel sorry for them" than in the ape house. Sorry, zebras, snakes, marmosets, and camels. Sorry, lions and bats. You're all going to have to learn how to eat, frown, or masturbate like humans do before they waste a moment of their day pitying your captivity. We humans are a narcissistic species; we look for ourselves in everything.

As I turn to escape the crowd, a little boy runs smack into my knees and apologizes, "Sorry, sir."

His mother quickly corrects him, "Ma'am," and ushers her son toward the glass so he can get a better look at monkeys doing what monkeys do.

"Isn't that the movie about the lady with the monkeys?" my mother asked.

It was 1993. I was sixteen. I'd faked sick that day to stay home from school, smoke copious amounts of marijuana, and channel surf. Mid-afternoon, I stumbled upon the movie *Gorillas in the Mist* and for the first time in my young life, a narrative resonated with me: *woman demands job, woman gets job, woman does not marry, woman does not live in quiet desperation, woman saves a species, woman is decapitated by unknown assailant, cue triumphant music.*

"Gorillas," I corrected her. "It's about gorillas."

I asked my mother to rent the movie.

"I need it for school," I lied.

My mother was skeptical. "They watched that in school? Am I thinking of the right movie?"

"Yes," I insisted. *"Gorillas in the Mist.* They watched it in Biology."

"Isn't Biology the class you and that Josephine skipped?"

I bristled at her use of "that Josephine," but having anticipated this response, bowed my head remorsefully and replied, "Yes."

The afternoon for which we'd earned the now infamous detention, Josephine and I had gone to the forest preserve. It was an unwritten rule that girls did not go there alone. Men sold drugs in the parking lots, women had been raped. The preserve was bifurcated by the narrowest end of the Des Plaines River, and that day we walked along the water, smoking cigarettes, shuffling our feet for the crunch of twigs and leaves, seeking things to touch. When Josephine spotted a frog on the bank, she shrieked then dared me to catch him.

"He doesn't want to be caught," I said.

"But I want him," she said, planting kisses on my cheek.

The frog took another leap onto a partially submerged rock.

"Forget it," Josephine said. "Now it's too late."

I kicked off my boots. The mud at the bank was cold. I glanced back at Josephine, her hands cupped over her mouth, eyes wide.

As I lunged forward, clapping my hands around the slimy body, I heard Josephine's wild laughter.

I slid back to her, the slick amphibian struggling in spasms, pulsing like a heart in my hands.

At the bank Josephine flinched, backed up.

"Here," I said.

One of the frog's legs loosed itself from my grip and punched at the air.

"I didn't think you'd actually do it," Josephine said, wincing. "He probably has diseases."

All my mother knew was that *that Josephine* was a bad influence. Had she known the full scope of my attachment to *that Josephine*, I would have been back in Catholic school. Public high school was a privilege, not a right.

My mother rented *Gorillas in the Mist* for me and before it was returned, I rigged up our households' two VCRs and made a pirate copy. When watching the movie wasn't enough, I took to skipping evenings out with friends at Denny's, choosing instead to spend my nights at the library scrolling through reel after reel of microfiche, checking out Dian Fossey biographies and books on primatology that hadn't been touched since the Nixon Administration.

I became a real smoker, first Marlboro Reds, because that's what Sigourney-Weaver-as-Dian-Fossey smoked, then Merit Lights when I learned those were what the actual Dian Fossey smoked. I listened to Billie Holiday, because that's what Sigourney-Weaver-as-Dian-Fossey listened to, but gave up Holiday for Edith Piaf when I read that she was who the actual Dian Fossey preferred.

Lucky for me, it was the early 1990s, and I didn't have to alter my fashion sense to fit Fossey's—save for the Doc Martens, I already dressed like her: tattered blue jeans and oversized flannel shirts.

Josephine felt threatened. "Do you love me?"

"Yes."

"But do you love me more than Dian Fossey?"

I'd laugh dismissively, placating her with, "Give me a break, I don't even know Dian Fossey," or "That's not a fair question: Dian Fossey is dead."

My parents were baffled by my obsession: "That movie? Again?"

My grandmother—who, whenever tipsy, would bitterly remind us that her family once owned all the land between Lincoln, Lawrence, and Western—now spent her third dirty martini openly fretting that I would skip college and hightail it to the Virungas. "You think they want white women there, Allison? Let me tell you, they do not."

For my seventeenth birthday, gifts included one of Jane Goodall's chimpanzee tomes, a sweatshirt with a gorilla's face emblazoned across the front, and a lemur hand puppet. But they didn't understand my obsession. It wasn't about apes. It was about courage, causes; being unwelcome somewhere but standing your ground.

Prior to the ubiquity of cell phones and the advent of the internet, teenagers managed to communicate clandestinely through the night. Josephine and I devised a code:

two rings and a hang up meant "call me"; *one ring and a hang up* meant "come over."

Josephine's family lived in a one-story ranch, where her bedroom faced the street. When she rang once, I would sneak out, drive the Dodge Omni my parents loaned me to Josephine's street, park two blocks from her house, walk up her front lawn and tap lightly on her window; she'd raise the frame, pop out the screen, and I would climb inside. By the time we graduated from high school, I'd been climbing through that window so long I could scale the wall and slip through like a pole-vaulter.

We got away with a lot because our parents were worried about our brothers. My younger brother was a burgeoning stoner-pyromaniac, while Josephine's older brother, Kyle, was forever being suspended from school for calling teachers "cocksuckers" and punching students in the halls.

Kyle was a nineteen-year-old senior who stormed about Josephine's house perpetually shirtless, arms and chest muscular in a way I'd only ever seen in action movies. When he wasn't lying in the driveway, swearing and tinkering with the Mustang he would never fix, Kyle was in the basement lifting weights or locked in his bedroom blasting Nitzer Ebb: *muscle and hate/muscle and hate/muscle, muscle, muscle . . .*

On the outside of Kyle's bedroom door hung a Confederate flag underscored by a black bumper sticker that read: *AIDS Kills Fags Dead.*

On my way back from the zoo, riding the Clark Bus, I watch my reflection in the window: *ten-pounds overweight, bug-eyed dyke with a bad haircut.* I try to see the "sir" the little boy saw when he ran into my legs, and I can't. I try to see the "ma'am" his mother saw, and I can't see that either.

The bus rolls past the old German Catholic cemetery where my grandmother is buried. She can no longer fear my escape to Africa, and as the bus moves alongside the walled graveyard, I silently assure her I am not in the depths of some lawless jungle, *I am here, somewhere between Lincoln, Lawrence, and Western.*

"Chicago went to hell in the seventies," my grandmother used to say. "At least the suburbs are safe."

But the suburbs never seemed safe to me. My inner city Chicago was African American, Puerto Rican, Jewish, Ethiopian, Mexican, Korean, Polish, German, Somalian, poor and rich, writers and working class, dykes, fags, trannies and lunatics—and in this way, the city felt safer to me than the suburbs, where the slightest difference—a tattoo, an accent, a particular haircut—rendered one a freak. In the suburbs, Josephine and I were peculiar, but peculiar together; we made a city unto ourselves.

Josephine and I sat in her parents' living room watching *Gorillas in the Mist.* Regarding myself as something of a Dian Fossey scholar, I critiqued the film pompously.

"Now her tracker's name wasn't really Sembagare."

"There was no such zoo broker—all Hollywood."

During the one sex scene in the movie, I shifted uncomfortably, protesting, "Dian Fossey would never say that."

Josephine inched closer to me. "What *would* Dian Fossey say?"

Even at seventeen, I recognized this as a skill, and was amazed at the ease with which Josephine could segue into flirtation, and fluster me. Moreover, how brazenly she did this—in the school cafeteria, in restaurants, in her parents' living room.

"What would Dian Fossey say?" she prodded, laughing.

Before I could answer, Kyle, wearing nothing but American flag biker shorts, stomped past us, bare chest sweating from bench presses, shouting, "Faggot niggers fucking monkeys is where we got AIDS."

Wielding the remote control, Josephine jumped up onto the couch. "What the fuck, Kyle?" she screamed. "What is your fucking problem?"

I pulled at her pant leg. He didn't know about us, and I wanted to keep it that way. "Forget it," I whispered. "Just let it go."

Josephine launched the remote at Kyle's head, but her aim was off and it broke open against the wall. Before he ducked into his bedroom, Kyle paused and put up two middle fingers—one for each of us.

When Kyle made Josephine's home feel unsafe, we started hanging out in the city with Brian. Josephine had worked with Brian in the video store. He was twenty-five, had long auburn hair, and tattoo sleeves depicting dragons and naked women; he was the coolest guy we knew.

Brian took me and Josephine to a bar on Armitage where the bartenders let us drink, where Josephine made me dance, where they played the kind of music we liked: Jane's Addiction, Fugazi, Joy Division. None of our other high school friends got to hang out in the city and drink.

One night at the bar, I watched Brian's roommate don a clown wig and snort a line of coke off a woman's thigh.

Later, I watched Brian grab Josephine and kiss her on the mouth. When I saw her kiss back, I drank myself sick.

Josephine followed me into the stall, holding my hair back as I retched. From the jukebox, Ian MacKaye wailed: *I am a patient boy/I wait/I wait/I wait . . .*

"I want to go home," I said.

Josephine stroked my head. "Al," she said. "It's the nineties. He's just some guy. You can't take everything so seriously."

"I *will* take everything seriously," I slurred. "Dian Fossey took everything seriously, and she's a fucking legend. *A legend . . .*"

I *was* serious, and a little self-righteous, and though I believed this was a kind of courage, Josephine laughed, as she so often did, right in my face.

She drove us home in the Dodge, and I spent the trip thinking about that scene in *Gorillas in the Mist* when Sigourney-Weaver-as-Dian-Fossey yells, "Get off my mountain!" and imagined myself screaming something similar to Brian, and to Kyle. By the time we pulled up outside Josephine's house, I was so enraged I couldn't look her in the eye. She went inside and waited for me to come tapping at the window.

I never did.

Two weeks before high school graduation, Josephine gave me a spider figurine. The spade-shaped body was made of crystal, the spindly legs sterling silver. I understood the significance immediately. Josephine was absurdly afraid of spiders, and the first time we slept together, I had "saved her" from a daddy longlegs crawling across the wall beside her bed, catching it with my bare hands and tossing it out the window despite her directive to "Kill it! Kill it!"

Fond of such symbolic gestures, Josephine said, "I gave this to you because you aren't afraid of anything."

I scoffed. I was afraid of everything. I was afraid of her and her unpredictable affection, her reckless love. I was afraid of the myriad ways she was utterly unlike me. Studying the crystal spider in my hands, I wasn't sure what it was we had that I was supposed to defend.

That night, as I left through Josephine's window, the porch light came on. This had never happened before. Figuring her parents had installed new sensors, and fearing recognition, I pulled my sweatshirt's hood over my head.

As I walked across the front lawn, I heard footsteps and before I could think to run, I was on my stomach. The grass smelled sharp and tasted of chemicals. I couldn't catch my breath. A vice tightened around my waist; an incredible weight bore down on my spine.

"Kyle," I screamed. "Kyle, it's me!"

Kyle rolled me over and yanked down my hood. "What the fuck are you doing?"

I couldn't answer. He stood and swiped grass and dirt from his legs. I blinked dumbly; the vision in my right eye was blurred, and as I attempted to straighten my glasses, my nose began to bleed.

In an uncharacteristic gesture of mercy, Kyle held out his hand to help me up. Once I was on my feet, he yanked the hand away. "Get the fuck out of my face."

I walked, stunned, to the Dodge. Inside the car, I flipped down the mirror. The entire right side of my face was red and blue beneath a grass stain veneer. My upper lip was mustached with blood. When I tried to correct the severe tilt of my glasses, one arm broke off the frame and I began to sob. I drove home with one hand shaking on the wheel, the other holding my frames to my face like opera glasses.

My favorite part in *Gorillas in the Mist* was when Dian Fossey intercepts Claude Van Vecten in his van. When confronted by Fossey, Van Vecten laughs in her face, and she grabs his meaty hand with its ostentatious gold ring: "You like this ring? You want to keep the hand this ring is on? If I ever hear, or see, or smell you anywhere near my gorillas, you'll be wearing that ring on the other hand, and I'll have a new ashtray."

Driving home that night, I imagined how I'd grip Kyle's balls in my hand like a panicked frog: *If I ever see, or hear, or smell you anywhere near me, you'll be stuffing your bike shorts, and I'll have a new bookmark.* But the idea of fighting for myself, much less Josephine, terrified me. Kyle had downed me like a domino; all my best comebacks were borrowed lines. Josephine didn't want my heroics. She probably wanted Brian, or some other boy, so I never told her about Kyle. I just stopped going to their house.

Getting off the bus, I decide on a Sunday evening drink at the neighborhood dyke bar, Stargaze. I text a friend. "I feel like going out," I type. "I feel like going to Stargaze."

"You can't," she replies. "They've closed."

I experience a moment of incredulity. "Where are the dykes supposed to go?"

"Anywhere we want," she writes. "Regular bars."

"True," I agree. "We can be lesbians anywhere now."

Out is in.

After high school, I went away to college at a liberal arts school in Wisconsin. It was still the 1990s: Ellen Degeneres hadn't yet come out, Clinton's "don't ask don't tell" seemed progressive, the idea of "tolerance" was downright radical, and I was quietly, openly gay on campus—protected by liberal friends and professors.

It's easy to be brave when you feel safe.

Josephine skipped college and moved into a dodgy part of the West Loop with Adrian, a handsome Puerto Rican who made a little money spinning records in nightclubs and a lot of money dealing ecstasy and heroin.

My freshman year, I took the train in from Wisconsin to visit her and Adrian at the apartment they shared. Josephine apologetically explained that Adrian was more than "just her roommate," but I knew that already. I wasn't hurt. I was relieved.

Life, it seemed, had fallen into a sort of "natural order" for us both. Josephine had her reckless city life, and I had my books and tepid activism in Kenosha, Wisconsin. In early adulthood, with our first taste of real agency, neither of our chosen paths was particularly noble or interesting or brave.

At her apartment, we smoked cigarettes, reminisced about high school and how good it was to be out of the suburbs. I waxed arrogant about my newest obsession, Anne Sexton, quoted her: *Live or die, but don't poison everything...* I had dumped Fossey and her dumb gorillas, found a new chain-smoking alcoholic to admire, and set my sights on becoming a poet.

Josephine was addicted to heroin, but I ignored this

fact, justifying my disregard by misappropriating a line from a Roethke poem: *I, with no rights in this matter,/ Neither father nor lover.*

I ran my hands over her and Adrian's couch, scabbed with cigarette burns, and asked, "How did you manage this?"

Josephine squinted defensively, "Never burned a hole in your couch before, Smokey?"

I dropped the subject and stared at my hands. For the rest of the evening and into the morning, I ignored the small bunches of foil scattered throughout the apartment. Pretended the hypodermic needle lying in the bathroom sink was a glimpse of something else—a silverfish, a hairpin. I told myself Josephine's weight loss and strange acne were from waitressing too much.

"You look tired," I observed, gently, as we readied for bed.

Josephine gathered up beer bottles. Every time she leaned forward, her shoulder blades poked against the back of her t-shirt like clipped wings. She swept stray ash from the coffee table into her hands. "It looks like a zoo in here," she said. "It's like that movie."

"Huh?" I knew what she meant, but wasn't in the mood for nostalgia.

Josephine looked hurt. "That gorilla movie," she said, too stoned to remember the title.

I raised my eyebrows, smirked, "'Gorilla movie?'"

"Yeah," she said, poking me, and I flinched, backed away. She seemed not to notice, and closing her eyes, absent-mindedly quoted a line from the film; a quiet line delivered toward the end of the movie. In the scene, Fossey sits in her cabin with her faithful tracker, Sembagare, stringing popcorn to hang on the Christmas tree. Sembagare chastises her for shooting at tourists, and Fossey, looking small and spent, drops her popcorn garland, lights a cigarette and declares, "They're not going to turn this mountain into a goddamn zoo. They're not."

Music in the Head

music sees more than I.
I mean, it remembers better;
remembers that first night here.
It was the strangled cold of November;
even the stars were strapped to the sky
and the moon too bright
forking through to stick me
with a singing in the head.

—ANNE SEXTON, "MUSIC SWIMS BACK TO ME"

After four months of non-stop rock 'n' roll, my father disappeared. While he was gone, we stayed with my grandparents. For three weeks, my brother and I slept side-by-side on blanket beds in my grandfather's study; every night my long legs would catch under the desk and I'd dream dinosaurs were devouring me to the hip.

It was 1988, a recession year. My father had just lost his job that afforded our family the big house in the suburbs, the red Cadillac with leather interior, the condo on Sanibel Island. Prior to the recession, my father had been aggressively thrifty. In spite of our upper-middle class financial status, my father used empty dog food bags to pack his lunch, added water to shampoo bottles to make that quarter ounce of Head & Shoulders last a little longer; he darned his socks, made our peanut butter and jelly sandwiches on hotdog buns if we were out of regular bread.

Now, strapped with superfluous expenses he couldn't afford, my father behaved in a curious manner. Instead of looking for a new job, instead of reigning in the budget, he began spending money. Copiously. He bought a computer when computers were still expensive novelties; he bought a new stereo for the living room (one with a CD player); he bought a television as wide as our couch and a van a little bigger than the television that had a television inside.

And then there was music.

It felt like we weren't only getting better stuff, we were getting a better father.

My father had once liked music the way people who wouldn't consider themselves drinkers might like a cocktail when they go out to dinner. He wasn't like me, didn't need music every day, didn't want to learn to play instruments, didn't seek out new bands or attend concerts.

In early adolescence, I began stealing my father's records—slipping them from their shelf under the living room stereo and smuggling them into my bedroom. Door closed, I'd play them as loud as my little record player would allow. I felt I had discovered a black magic—if I was angry, music was angrier. If I was sad, music was sadder. If I was happy, music was happier. Music made perfect sense, and yet it made no sense at all—I was in love.

My mother also owned records, but I never stole them. I didn't care for my mother's record collection, called the music she listened to "J-Music" because my mother's name began with a "J" and because most of the singers she liked also had names beginning with "J": Janis Ian, Judy Collins, Joni Mitchell.

My father's music was just better: Creedence Clearwater Revival, Booker T. & the M.G.'s, The Animals, The Rolling Stones, Count Five, Elvis. My father's music was meant to be played loudly and recklessly, whereas my mother's music was best enjoyed at a reasonable volume while crying secret tears into a glass of chardonnay.

After he lost his job, my father started listening to music almost all of the time.

I'm a monkeeeey man, Mick Jagger screeched at midnight.

It ain't me, it ain't me, John Fogerty wailed at six in the morning.

Many nights, I'd sleep with a pillow folded around my head to drown out Jimmy Hendrix shredding his guitar in the living room.

One Saturday morning, I awoke to Marvin Gaye crooning something about taxes, which wasn't so bad because it was smooth and I could almost sleep through it. Then Marvin stopped abruptly, and in his place was my mother's voice. "Enough!" she yelled. "What the *fuck* is the matter with you?"

I sat up in bed. I had never heard my mother say "fuck" before, and the word made matters seem frighteningly serious. That day my father borrowed my Walkman and never gave it back.

A few weeks later, my father lay in bed listening to music for five uninterrupted hours. Afterwards my parents fought, and I heard my father weeping. I heard him tell my mother he knew the meaning of life, "And it's not money."

"Tell me, then," she said, caustically. "Tell me what it is."

"Music," he said. "It's music."

When I got home from school that day, my father was gone.

Soon after my father's first hospitalization, Tipper Gore successfully lobbied to have warning labels placed on all the albums that contained so-called "suggestive lyrics," and at fourteen, I learned the meaning of the word "censorship"; in being opposed to it, I found my very first political cause.

Hostage to my parents' money and my mother's discretion, it seemed every album I wanted wore that little black and white badge—*Parental Advisory: Explicit Lyrics*.

"I'm not buying you anything dirty," my mother would say, frowning and pushing my selection away.

"It's not dirty," I'd protest. "It just has some swears."

"What swears?"

"I don't know. I haven't heard the whole thing yet."

"If you haven't heard it, why do you want it so badly?"

In those moments, I despised Tipper Gore with every fiber of my being.

Ms. Gore would later lobby on behalf of those with mental illnesses, and after spending the better part of my adolescence and teenage years telling friends and family that my father was being repeatedly hospitalized for strokes and heart problems (because, though deadly, those afflictions were less embarrassing), all the while being denied seriously good rock music, I grew to have tremendously conflicted feelings about Tipper Gore.

When my father returned from hospital, all references to mental illness were banned. Phrases like "that's nuts," "what a psycho," and "crazy," phrases absolutely entrenched in the teenage gestalt, were rendered taboo. My mother received slip-ups with all the disapproving-eyebrow-arching previously reserved for the infrequent "son of a bitch" and "fuck." For a time, it seemed my mother would rather my brother and I run through the house screaming "cocksucking motherfucker" than dare describe someone we disliked as "mental."

Not until all references to mental illness were forbidden did I realize how many there were, especially in music.

I'm crazy for cryin'/and crazy for lyin'/and I'm crazy for lovin' you—
I'm goin' off the rails of the crazy train—
Oh little girl, psychotic reaction—
Jungle love is drivin' me mad/makin' me crazy—
Let's go crazy, let's get nuts—
Manic depression is touchin' my soul—

Medicated and done with music, my father started his own company that did contract work for NASA and Boeing. The business was successful, in large part, because my father was a brilliant engineer. Engineering, for my father, was not merely his occupation; it was the way in which he saw the world. He spoke a foreign language of numbers, circuits, maps, and mechanical anatomies. According to my father, anything that was real, that was actual, could be represented numerically, diagrammed, scribbled out in code.

As a kid, I once watched my father make an air filter to suck the cigarette smoke out of the garage (where he spent the vast majority of his time) using a soldering iron, a circuit board, and a broken box fan. He could turn the useless into essential machinery. He could fix anything. Sometimes, neighbors would bring broken items to my father's garage—once a lawnmower, once a television set, once a kid's musical jewelry box—and my father would make them functional again.

I remember the jewelry box because it belonged to a girl I despised. I was angry that he was fixing something of hers. "Maybe it can't be fixed," I suggested, hopefully.

A cigarette dangling from his lips, he tweaked a spring that twirled the ballerina and she spun again. "It's easy," he grumbled. "Way easier than makin' a missile detector."

Though my father's business did well, he talked a lot, that first year out of the hospital, about his hatred for Ronald Reagan and Reagan's successor, George Bush. My father blamed Reagan for the loss of his "safer, steadier" job within a company he wasn't responsible for running. To this day, when I hear someone say something kind about Ronald Reagan, I am the first to insist he was a bastard, the first to cite his handling (or lack thereof) of the AIDS crisis, the Iran-Contra scandal, the birth of the fundamentalist neo-con. In fact, the mere mention of the former president makes my heart pound.

It took me many years to parse my Reagan-aversion. I don't really remember Iran-Contra. I only remember see-ing Oliver North perpetually swearing-in. When AIDS was the lead news story, I was a little girl in Catholic school, where the nuns told us AIDS wasn't something we should worry about unless we planned to have sex with monkeys or grow up to be homosexual men.

Why I really hate Reagan is that on some primal, irrational level, I blame him for making my father sick.

The summer before my senior year in college, my brother called me with an ominous warning, "Dad's listening to music."

Sure enough, when my father picked me up at my Wisconsin campus, he was manic—told me a dirty joke, told me he was thinking of building an airplane, told me he was writing poetry. On the drive home to Illinois, I sat on my hands, chewed my lips, tried to believe he was just happy.

My father drove so fast that we hit and killed a bird flying across the highway. Until then, I didn't think it was possible to hit a bird in flight, but we did—a sparrow. When its body thumped against the windshield, my father didn't flinch. A thread of blood ribboned from its beak and my father flicked on the windshield wipers, swiped the bird from the car, turned up the music: Neil Diamond.

Sweet Caroline!

Good times never felt so good...

My father glanced at me, laughed at my alarm, and sang willfully along.

Seven years after his first episode, my father returned to the hospital on my twenty-first birthday. That night I went to a bar with friends. The Verve had just released "Bittersweet Symphony" and the androgynous pre-pubescent Mormons, "MMMbop." But that night, at the bar, the DJ only played 70s disco.

A group of men from the nearby naval station, still in their crisp white uniforms, bought us girls multiple shots of fluorescent booze served in test tubes.

When I was drunk enough, I danced to "Don't Leave Me This Way" with a skinny sailor who pulled me in close and said, "You look just like Liza Minnelli."

The compliment made me queasy—queen of jazz hands, rhapsodic sentimentality, and the belting of Broadway show tunes. The only link in that moment between Liza Minnelli and myself was that I was drunk.

My father would get better for short periods of time and lose interest in music. And then he would get worse again and return to music. And then he would get better, and then he would get worse. And then there was music, and then there was no music. As the Buddhists and Donovan say, "First there is a mountain, then there is no mountain, then there is."

The summer I turned thirty, my mother moved out.

When I learned that my mother had packed up her Janis Ian, Joni Mitchell, Judy Collins and rented an apartment, I was in Ireland—a country that speaks, almost exclusively, in ballads.

The news didn't come as a surprise. My father had been sick for months. Not only was he listening to music, he was painting murals on the walls, had bought a vacation home he could not afford, was endeavoring to trace his lineage back to Jesus Christ.

A cancer patient seldom argues the diagnosis. A cancer patient does not say, "Well, maybe cancer is just the way I'm supposed to be." A cancer patient does not debate each doctor who tells him, "You have cancer."

The tumors, the lesions, the fatigue cannot be denied. The proof is manifest. For my father, there was never enough real evidence. A man of science, he could not believe in, could not respect, anything that couldn't be proven at the cellular or atomic level. My father placed psychology in the same category as astrology, and the euphoria his illness afforded him in no way fit with his idea of a symptom.

When my mother left, my father started purchasing things impulsively—software, hardware, books, art, but mostly music. Sometimes, visiting him, I would pull into the driveway and hear music vibrating through the garage door.

My father's music collection grew to rival my own. He seldom went to work, spent his days in the garage indulging in everything from Stravinsky to Snoop Dogg.

On his worst days, he stayed home from work and called me at odd hours of the night. "You ever hear of this band, Nirvana?"

"Yeah, dad, like fifteen years ago."

In these moments, I wanted so badly to feel sympathy for my sad, sick father, but all I could think was: *Damn you*.

Nirvana. *Nevermind*. I could still remember the first time I heard that album—those holy opening chords, the explosive rush of drums. The first time I heard *Nevermind*, I knew I needed a whole new group of friends, a whole new identity, a whole new life.

I feel stupid and contagious/here we are now/entertain us—

Sixteen years later, in a single phone call after midnight on a Tuesday, my father polluted the memory, caused me to forever associate the band, the album, with his madness.

Hitler ostensibly tainted Wagner. Marilyn Manson was blamed for the massacre at Columbine. Quoting lyrics in her habit as we blushed fiercely, Sister Enid lectured my fourth grade class on the evils of the pop song, "Boom Boom (Let's Go Back to My Room)." On New Year's Eve, 1982, in my favorite taffeta skirt and patent leather shoes, I danced with my father to "Rock Around the Clock"— a song that, after a 1958 incident at a Bill Haley concert in Berlin, was feared to incite riots. All beer breath and Old Spice, my father swung my hands back and forth and twirled me under his arms until I was dizzy and collapsing with laughter.

Some twenty years later, that same man called me at two a.m. to ask if I had "ever heard of Nirvana."

Music complicates our history, our sense of linearity, of certainty. Music speaks to the part of us that is perpetually confused, that asks, *How is it possible for this plane to fly?* Music communicates with the part that secretly thinks email is magic; the part that is irrationally frightened and hopeful, that finds connections that might not be there; the part that is blood raw, that must make an urgent two a.m. phone call to ask about a band.

In Ireland, the first summer my parents lived apart, I stayed at a friend's family home. The night I learned of their separation, after walking the mossy woods with the mangy, shit-stinking town dog, Bridie, I returned to the house to find my friend and her family sitting around the kitchen table drinking tea and singing songs. They did this every night, so I wasn't surprised. In fact, until the news of my parents' split, I had marveled at, and participated in, this ritual—after all, what but a bird sings every day?

But that night, instead of walking into the sing-a-long, I remained outside. I knew that if I went in, I would be made a cup of milky tea, made to sing my favorite Irish folk song: *Oh, Peggy Gordon, you are my darlin', come sit you down upon my knee*—and I wanted Peggy Gordon nowhere near me. Not on my knee, not in my throat.

I lit a cigarette, clapped my thigh for Bridie to come close, and together we walked up the road to a little stone bridge. Even in silence, the world was not still—ivy quivered as it climbed; fog drifted sluggishly over pastures; and clouds sped across the pale night sky, a sky that seemed bigger than any I'd seen before, an infinite absence coldly announced by the moon.

The disturbance came from sheep braying in the distance, those discordant human notes, calling to one another in the deep quiet.

President of Drama Club

In my early thirties, I experienced a renewed obsession with Virginia Woolf, re-reading her letters to Vita Sackville-West, devouring tedious biographies and regaling my friends with stories of Woolf's pranks, spats, and quirks. "Did you know the Woolfs had a pet monkey?!" But the trivia that really enthralled me concerned the fact that Woolf—though immersed in Bloomsbury's taboo-shattering, liberal bohemian culture—was very shy, a blusher. It was this detail that gave me what I was really after; a connection to Woolf, a flicker of recognition. For while I may not know what it is to be a genius, I do know, quite well, what it is to be a blusher.

It seldom happens anymore, but from childhood to my mid-twenties, I blushed constantly. One need only ask my name and I'd blush so hot I felt my hair might catch fire. Blushing is a horrible betrayal, rendering the blusher unable to disguise shame, discomfort, anxiety, or attraction because she wears these emotions fervidly on her face.

"You're blushing," people observed, as though I was unaware of the inferno raging from my neck to my cheekbones. Such observations only made the blushing intensify, until my entire face throbbed with heat.

The speculations around Woolf's blushing—"Profound sexual neuroses," "oppressive Victorian upbringing"—caused me to wonder at the origins of my own shyness. *Bad haircuts? Braces? Being the first girl in my class to need glasses and the last to need a bra?*

Whatever the origins, shyness is oppressive; you stay quiet when you know the answer, tremble when called upon, fear attention—even the attention you want. Shyness renders the sufferer a silent observer, an anonymous audience member forever stuck on the wrong side of the fourth wall.

Then there's the other ubiquitous metaphor: *You need to be brought out of your shell.* Let us, for a moment, consider the metaphor's implications; consider that to remove a turtle from its shell would be on par with removing a person's spine, ribs, and all the skin from their arms to their waist—in the fashion of Ed Gein. But the more important way this metaphor fails is that shyness is not a protective layer. Shyness is not a place to hide; shyness is the exposed state of *being hidden.*

My mother saw my freshman year in public high school as an opportunity for me to at long last wrest myself from that proverbial shell—spine, ribs, and all. I was an awkward, lonely kid; a nail-biter. My mother saw high-school as my do-over, my chance to cast off not just the shell, but the low rung social shackles that had bound me to the horse-head sketching and science-fair-project deliberating of Catholic school's nerd underworld.

At my old school they'd called me "Helen Keller" because I seldom spoke, "Kermit the Frog" for my long, skinny legs and big feet, "Gandhi" because I wore glasses with round frames. And while Helen Keller and Gandhi are admirable figures, no junior high girl wants to be likened to them.

After ten years of ridicule, I looked forward to the freedom afforded by public school—freedom from religion, freedom from uniforms, freedom from my monikers, "Kermit," "Mahatma."

Clothes, I knew, were the first piece in the puzzle of my own reinvention. For a decade, my clothing had been preordained. The clothes I wore on weekends—blue jeans and sweatshirts bearing the names of places I'd vacationed with my parents—seemed too childish. I liked the idea of torn jeans ("piranha pants," my mother called them) and rock t-shirts like the stoner kids wore. I also liked the idea of flowing skirts, bangles and scarves, something Stevie Nicks-y. But could I pull these things off? Could Helen Keller rock a Megadeth t-shirt? Could Kermit look cool in shredded denim?

But my mother had other things in mind. Brightly colored turtlenecks, cable-knit sweaters, khaki pants, ironed blue jeans. When I objected, she insisted the look was "cute," though I knew that "cute" was not an adjective that suited me. "Cute" was for girls with a bounce in their step, girls who wore flavored lip gloss and spent their weekends rendezvousing with boys at the mall. In the end, my reinvention didn't make me look "cute" so much as it made me look like a middle-aged suburban housewife.

Unfortunately I was fourteen, and my mother held the purse strings, so teal sweaters, pleated pants, a haircut replete with bangs and perm (and permed bangs) it would be. Fashion, however, wasn't the worst part of my mother's "Extreme Makeover: 1989 Edition." Rather, it was the social component of her master plan that felt like my undoing.

Extra-curricular activities were for people who liked to talk, who liked to laugh, who enjoyed playing charades and eating lukewarm pizza with strangers. I was so shy, I'd rather have imagined what it might be like to have friends than actually make any.

Want to sit in silence, perusing musty Brontë novels and listening to this old Simon & Garfunkel record?

Why yes, I'd like that very much.

Great. Can I offer you a beverage?

No, I'm fine with Jane Eyre.

At my mother's proposal, I whined and protested. During one of my chronic leg aches, I made a scene of taking an extra Advil as a passive aggressive suicidal gesture. My mother would have none of it. By the third week of freshman year, I was a member of Yearbook, Students for a Clean Earth (quite radical in '89), Band, Track, and—horror of horrors—Drama Club.

Yearbook and Students for a Clean Earth were my favorite groups, not because I cared about the causes, but because there were no tryouts—members just showed up and the meetings consisted of twenty freshmen listening to four or five upperclassmen discussing photo layout and recycling measures, respectively.

Band involved tryouts, and while I played the piano beautifully and clarinet horribly, the band director put me permanently on clarinet because, after all, clarinet is the instrumental sponsor of nerds, dorks, and geeks.

Like Band, Track also required tryouts. However, because they accepted me, the Track tryouts were clearly just a formality. I am not, nor have I ever been, athletically inclined, and at fourteen I was especially clumsy, too tall, too thin, and walked with a limp. I had nothing to contribute to the Track Team but comic relief.

Mortifying though Track and Band were, Drama Club—which did not require tryouts—felt far, far worse. Unlike Yearbook or Students for a Clean Earth, Drama Club meetings were designed to be wholly interactive; charades, monologues, and warm-up games where one conveyed emotional tone through recitation of a single word like "vacuum" or "slaughter."

My mother confused my hyperbole, histrionics, run-of-the-mill teenaged melodrama for acting talent, because I had no business being a member of Drama Club. People who joined Drama Club had aspirations of being seen, of being exposed in overwhelming states of emotion.

As a little girl I'd sung my grandparents musical numbers, things like "It's a Hard-Knock Life" and "Tomorrow." I'd obliged them because I could be hidden while I sang—under a blanket, behind a couch, beneath the kitchen table. They thought this was cute. "Here's an afghan," my grandmother would say. "Now sing 'Somewhere Over the Rainbow.'"

But without a decent hiding place, I did what I could in Drama Club to avoid participation: I sat at the back of the room, avoided eye contact, pretended to be immersed in abdominal breathing exercises.

At my first Drama Club meeting, I took some comfort in the discovery that the group was inhabited largely by nerds—*my people*. However, I quickly learned that Drama Club nerds were a particular species of dork, a branch from which I was not descended—the loud, overly-confident genus: *Nerdus Obnoxious*. The whole enterprise filled me with terror, and after that first day

I would have demanded an out, swallowed three Advil and locked myself in the bathroom all night, were it not for Becky Frank.

Oh, Becky Frank.

Becky Frank was the President of Drama Club; a tall, pale senior with long jet-black hair. She wore broomstick skirts, too much patchouli and many thin, jangling bracelets on both arms. Like so many members of Drama Club, Becky Frank was often loud and boisterous, but she could also be quiet, passively thoughtful. It was this dual nature that imbued Becky Frank with an air of mystery. Unlike the other members who were constantly chattering, guffawing, and hamming it up as though a moment of introspection would cause them to self-destruct, Becky Frank knew when to be silent.

That first semester, the high school put on a production of *Picnic*. As with all theater events, members of Drama Club were strongly encouraged to attend. I never felt compelled to do anything that my extra-curricular organizations *strongly encouraged,* but I did attend a performance of *Picnic* because Becky Frank was one of the leads.

Sitting there, in the cool darkness of the school's theater, safe in audience-anonymity, I studied Becky Frank, her beautiful black hair sprayed gray and knotted up in a bun, as she convincingly—so, so convincingly—begged Howard, a pimply sophomore in a bowler hat and bowtie, a man she couldn't possibly be attracted to, to marry her. I was awed. Becky could fake it, effortlessly. From floppy haired, Bohemian teenager—Birkenstocks and dream catcher earrings—to shrill, middle-aged schoolmarm in stiff wool. Becky Frank could transform. She was a genius.

I wanted desperately to tell Becky Frank that I thought her performance brilliant, to tell her she was *incomparable*—a word I'd once heard used in reference to Judy Garland. I wanted to give her flowers, to grab her and kiss her squarely on the mouth, to say, "You are divinely gifted and I love you madly." But when I saw her at the next Drama Club meeting, I couldn't even manage to say, "nice job," fearing my words would come out thin and stupid, fearing I would stammer or, worse yet, blush.

After seeing *Picnic,* Drama Club became my favorite extra-curricular activity. Drama Club was Becky Frank Club, a place for me to sit silently in a sea of animated nerds, sneaking furtive glances at my secret paramour, our fair president.

Drama Club was also my mother's favorite of all my involvements. Unlike Track, Band, and Yearbook, I didn't invent illnesses and protest on days when I had a Drama Club meeting. I suppose my mother took my lack of resistance to mean I'd caught the acting bug, as evidence that I'd changed, that her plan had succeeded. Perhaps my mother envisioned me someday tearfully accepting the Oscar, "I was once so painfully shy. If it weren't for my mom, I'd have never joined Drama Club."

At the end of the year, Becky Frank would graduate and Drama Club would need a new president. That Becky Frank would graduate filled me with tremendous anxiety and sorrow. It also made me certain that, come sophomore year, I would no longer attend Drama Club. A Drama Club without Becky Frank held no meaning.

As the year progressed, and Becky Frank's departure loomed larger, I began to despair openly. One night, after my mother asked about Drama Club, instead of delivering the usual petulant "fine" or "not much," I made the mistake of mentioning that we would soon be voting on a new President.

My mother's eyes widened. "Who will be the new president?" she asked.

"Whoever wants to be, I guess."

"Do you want to be?"

"No," I said. "I don't."

However, at the following meeting of Drama Club, when around the room like an ugly baby was passed the sign-up sheet for Drama Club president nominees, it occurred to me that all a nominee had to do was write a speech. More importantly, on the day of the speeches, Becky Frank would hear what the nominee had written.

I did not want to win; I only wanted Becky Frank to hear my words, for Becky Frank to sit rapt, intrigued by the quiet freshman who rose to the podium and delivered a brilliant, poignant speech. I imagined Becky Frank, her mouth agape in wonder, so still her bracelets fell silent, marveling, "Great Scott! Who is this quiet genius? And why have I not spoken to her before?" At best, Becky Frank would want to be friends with me. At worst, for a few shining moments, I would be the center of Becky Frank's attention, a thought in her mind.

Clouded with delusions of grandeur, I carefully printed my name on the sheet of yellow legal paper affixed to the clipboard. Passing the sign-up sheet along, I began to struggle with what I had done. I was filled with a mixture of dread, excitement, regret and profound inspiration— the very four emotions that would forever infuse my writing life.

That night, home from Drama Club, before my mother could ask, I bitterly announced, "I'm going to do it. I hope you're happy." The bitterness, of course, was an act. I could barely wait to get started on my masterpiece.

Upstairs in my bedroom, with a spiral-bound notebook and a blue pen, I began my composition.

Members of Drama Club...

It seemed to me that all major texts were inspired by love—love of country, of freedom, of God, of Becky Frank—and feeling myself part of this tradition, I chose my words carefully, knowing nations were built on the right synonym, dogma rested on a conjunction, the affections of a girl were earned with an adjective.

Though a freshman, I can assure you...

I read the piece aloud. I revised. I consulted the thesaurus. I painstakingly printed, by hand, my edits, and then, on a heavy old typewriter lugged from the basement, triumphantly hammered out my final copy.

In closing, I would like to acknowledge the efforts of our outgoing President, Becky Frank...

Like God himself, I labored for six days and on the seventh day rested, having arrived at what I deemed the perfect incarnation of my thoughts as to why I, who in no way wanted to be President of Drama Club, should absolutely and inarguably be President of Drama Club. To this day, that speech remains the most beautiful, most heartfelt piece of bullshit I have ever crafted.

The night of the Contender's Speeches, I was practically euphoric. I considered the degree to which Becky Frank would be impressed. I hoped she would not be rendered speechless, because I did want her to speak to me.

But as Drama Club gathered that night, Becky Frank was nowhere to be seen.

"Sick," I heard someone say.

"Running late," said someone else.

"She doesn't care, she's off to Northwestern in a few months," said another.

It was the latter comment that deflated me. My face blanched: *Becky Frank will not be here because Becky Frank doesn't care.*

One by one, the other candidates, all upperclassmen, approached the podium and delivered their poorly composed speeches, promising things that were simply not possible: *a new theater, advertisements in the Chicago Tribune, t-shirts for this year's fundraiser instead of last year's plain and peanut M&M's . . .*

Thinking Becky Frank a woman of character, of virtue, I had made no promises of "things." My speech was about big, noble concepts: *leadership, vision, opportunity.* I could see that I'd taken the process too seriously and was linguistically overdressed.

As my turn at the podium drew nearer, I contemplated a way out. I wanted a quilt to throw over my head. I wanted to race out the door. I wanted to quickly pencil in a talking point about peanut M&M's. But before I could plot an escape, my name was called.

In my pink turtleneck, with my perm and pleated khaki's, I rose to face Drama Club. I gazed out at a sea of overly-confident nerds—my people, but not my people—nerds in v-neck sweaters and "Don't Worry Be Happy" t-shirts, nerds in ripped blue jeans, nerds self-consciously licking their braces, snapping their gum, nerds shifting in their seats, nerds tired of listening to speeches.

My turtleneck felt tight around my throat. My hands sweat and shook. *Fuck you*, I thought. *Fuck you, Becky Frank.* My index cards fluttering in my hands, I delivered that son-of-a-bitch like my life depended on it. I enunciated. I gesticulated. Like a preacher in a hot church, I rendered that hoard of drama-geeks still and silent.

Afterwards, like all good orators, I went home and grimaced through a dinner of chicken and rice.

Later that evening, while I lay on my canopy bed, listening to Simon & Garfunkel and crying, the extraordinary happened. Becky Frank called the house.

I presumed Becky Frank was calling to apologize for being unable to attend the speeches, and before I said "hello," I resolved to forgive her, to accept her apology—casually, but graciously.

The reality of the phone call, however, was far, far worse: I was the new President of Drama Club.

"Just calling to congratulate you," Becky Frank said. "You won by a landslide."

I tried to sound happy, excited, but all I could muster was a muted, "Thanks."

"What's that?" asked Becky Frank.

"Thanks," I repeated.

"You should be excited," said Becky Frank. "President of Drama Club is dead; long live President of Drama Club."

As I hung up the phone, my father shook his head. "Whoever the hell that was, she mispronounced our last name."

Of course she did, I thought.

My mother's face beamed. "Did you win?"

I blushed fiercely. "No," I said. "There's nothing to win."

Silently, despondently, I made my way back to my bedroom.

Somewhere during my fourth listening of "I Am a Rock," I stopped sobbing and, struck by my success, began to gloat: I was President of Drama Club. I had never graced the stage and still I had been elected Becky's replacement based on the merit of my words. *Historically speaking,* I thought, *a talent such as yours is powerful, dangerous.*

I'd never play Rosemary in *Picnic* or deliver a monologue from *Our Town,* and I'd never be able to mime "eating soup." For the rest of my life, I'd tremble and blush whenever the spotlight shone on me. But I could write.

In the quiet, white room of the page, I could write beyond my purple face, could string together words that were clearer and more resonant than my voice would ever be. I could use this trait or talent or whatever it was I possessed to find the right people, my people; as Woolf says of solitude, "I thought how unpleasant it is to be locked out; and I thought how it is worse, perhaps, to be locked in." I fell asleep that night plotting to politely abdicate my Drama Club throne and sign up with the black-clad weirdos in Poetry.

Iowa

Life turned hopeless to the tune of "I Love the Flower Girl;" one minute I was sitting on my bed, doodling over math homework, and the next I was enveloped in despair, as though a thick net had been dropped on me.

By the time I was an adult, I was so accustomed to the experience I could almost hear the sucking sound in my head before everything blanched. I called these pale days "the sads." As an adult, the hardest part of having "the sads" was doing the ordinary things. The grocery store was the epicenter of hard normalcy, hideous utility; the Muzak death fugue, the lights casting their cruel fluorescence over milk, cereal, detergent.

I'd leave with one item only: canned soup. A ration, sustenance of the depressed. That was when I knew it was bad, when I knew it was time to go to Iowa.

Visiting Iowa as a kid, my cousins and I would roam the woods surrounding Uncle Ray's house, daring the boys to piss on the electric fence; at Aunt Cathy's, we chased each other through the nearby field marked "No Trespassing: Will Shoot;" we teased animals, blew things up. We put spins on classic games like hide-and-seek by adding the elements of mousetraps and M-80s, so the game was as much about hiding as it was about resilience.

Iowa always felt like an escape—a place where it was perfectly acceptable to wear blue jeans to church, swear in front of the children, smoke cigarettes in the kitchen and feed table scraps to the raccoons. My father, too, saw Iowa as an escape. He came here when he was sick—disappearing in the night once the threat of another hospital stay had been deployed. In Iowa, he hid out with his brother, his sisters, his mother—a fugitive on the run from his family in Illinois.

My relatives do not, by and large, believe in psychology. Like my father, each one is skeptical of doctors and the drugs they prescribe. Of my father's manic episodes, most say, "He's under a lot of stress." When conducting genealogical research, I found evidence of ancestors on that side of the family who died in rural lunatic asylums, who blew their brains out in woodsheds because of "stress." I'd researched my past hoping for a little royal ancestry, or a distant link to someone with brief, sparkling fame. The truth, however, was that I came from a long line of people who were impoverished and mentally ill. Though I struggled with "the sads," spent hours taking myself apart like a watch, spinning the gears, reassembling, setting myself to days of blankets and wall-gazing until I was moving clockwise again, I understood my malaise as ordinary; vastly different from my father's illness.

Dad and I sped along Highway Twenty in silence, having exhausted all possibilities for conversation at the Mississippi River Bridge. We both lit cigarettes and I watched fields sprawl for miles in the dark, interrupted only by small houses that disappeared and reappeared like images in a flipbook. The smell of crops, combines, and manure was as comforting in its familiarity as white bread, black coffee, and clean socks.

The previous summer had been a rough one in Iowa. An F5 tornado sent my cousin Michael's newly built house splintering across the tri-state area. My step-grandfather dropped dead—in front of my grandmother—during a routine doctor's appointment. Three weeks later, her home was destroyed by a flood.

My aunts shoveled mud, mice, sewage, garter snakes, and earthworms from what was once my grandmother's kitchen, living room, bathroom, bedroom. My father and uncles dragged drowned deer carcasses from the putrid, brown expanse that was now my grandmother's back-yard. Certain family members talked about the end of the world—The Bible, Nostradamus, the Mayans—as if to suggest this stretch of bad luck was divine prophecy, as if to suggest that among Nostradamus' predictions was a cryptic message about how the end shall come when the House of Gruber falls, as symbolized by short, bearded men smoking Merit Ultra Lights while hauling dead deer from an old woman's garden.

As a kid, it scared me when they talked like this. As an adult, I learned to dismiss it: *Protestants.* This particular summer there were no real tragedies to speak of. One of my cousin's kids set the curtains on fire, a beloved old dog died, Uncle Ray shot his hand clear through with a nail gun.

My father and I turned onto Sycamore Lane, the hilly gravel road that leads to Uncle Ray's house, a road onto which one is welcomed by a large yellow sign reading, "End County Maintenance"—and ain't it the truth. The lane snakes deep into the woods, dead-ends at my uncle's driveway, a driveway rendered useless by the four inoperable cars that occupy the space; cars that, in Aunt Trudy's words, "Ray will one day never fix."

Because there is no parking available in the driveway, one must park in what, I suppose, would constitute a front yard, negotiate space between trees, discarded propane tanks, broken lawnmowers, chicken wire, firewood, old tires, and hunks of scrap metal, all the while being careful not to hit one of the many dogs my aunt and uncle own, or drive off into the ditch that borders the lane.

Once we had yard-parked, my father and I made our way to the house, finding Uncle Ray, Aunt Trudy, and my cousin Annie sitting on the back deck, watching a standing tree burn in the woods.

"Didn't need to light the tree on fire," my father joked. "We woulda found the place."

Only Annie laughed.

Uncle Ray licked a rolled cigarette, leaned forward, stuck it in his mouth. He looked like a creased road map beside my neatly groomed father in his button-down shirt. Only their eyes were the same—wide and green, bulging above deep shadows. Their eyes were my eyes, the ones that friends affectionately called "wonk eyes," "bug eyes," or "ol' crazy eyes."

Uncle Ray stared intently at the tree, his nemesis du jour, then barked at my father, "Two. That fucker's been burning since two in the goddamn afternoon."

It was now nine at night. I looked at Annie; she shrugged.

"Call the fire department," I whispered to her.

"Fire department can't do shit," said Uncle Ray. "Can't get no water that far out on my goddamn property."

Then he told us that earlier that afternoon, he'd been burning a brush pile—weeds, garbage, broken furniture, flat tires—when a gust of wind came out of nowhere, blew an ember from the pile and carried it to the tree.

"Fucker went up in an instant," he said, both astonished and angry.

He lit another cigarette. "I tell you what I shoulda done. I shoulda felled that son of a bitch years ago. *Years ago.*"

All but Annie nodded. Her jaw set, she stared out into the woods, ran a hand through her thin, brown hair. She was thirty-eight. A debilitating genetic condition had kept her with Uncle Ray and Aunt Trudy all her life— she'd endured four decades of Uncle Ray's retrospect and was no longer amused.

I shoulda felled that son of a bitch years ago. Herein lies the paradox of my Iowa family's reasoning: accidents and disasters are both unforeseeable acts of God *and* purely predictable results of poor planning. I'd heard relatives apply the same logic to my father.

"This is just who he is," some would say.

And in the same breath, they'd add, "But if he didn't work so hard, this wouldn't happen."

As for the present situation, whether the tree burnt itself out or burnt down the woods and the house along with it, tomorrow my family would chalk up the outcome to divine intervention, part of God's plan. While the tree was burning, however, it was merely a failure of preparedness.

Uncle Ray told my father that in the moments before our arrival he'd grown increasingly concerned about the two giant limbs where the tree divided up top. "The crotch," he called it. Most of the tree's smaller branches had burned away, but *the crotch* obstinately remained— two red horns that at the slightest breeze spat fire into the forest. The sight was at once sinister and lovely.

I turned to my uncle. "But they'll burn off eventually, right?"

"Well, I put a couple slugs up there," he said. "Didn't seem to make a goddamn bit of difference."

"Slugs?"

Impassively, Annie schooled me. "Bullets," she said. "He shot the tree."

I blushed and looked away, then bit my lip to keep from laughing; shooting a burning tree felt on par with shooting at a flood or tornado, an act of absolute desperation, an act of someone unhinged, delusional.

This was the advantage of living in the woods, in the middle of nowhere. You could burn old clothes. You could shoot at a tree. You could cover yourself in kitten pelts and puppy blood and worship Satan. Life need not be ordinary.

A little after eleven, my father left the spectacle to spend the night at my grandmother's, where his bed would be made with clean sheets, where he'd get breakfast in the morning.

"Are you sure you don't want to come with?" he asked.

"No," I replied. "I'm good here."

Already the night was running against the sluggish, lukewarm current of normal life. I was wired, which felt better; if it meant a night in the back bedroom with taxidermied deer heads, and Aunt Trudy's dusty collection of porcelain angels, so be it.

My father left, Aunt Trudy went to bed, and Uncle Ray retreated sullenly indoors. Annie and I stayed on the deck, watching the tree emit plumes of rich wood smoke, schools of red dashes like demon minnows swimming into the forest.

When one of the tree's smaller branches cracked and, flame-engulfed, fell burning to the ground, Annie turned toward the house and, with all the dispassionate urgency of declaring "internet's down," announced, "branch came off." Her calm convinced me we would likely not burn alive—not tonight—and so I decided to get ready for bed. I gathered my toiletries and shuffled off to the bathroom. The sense of routine made my skin prickle with a familiar dread.

After a few minutes I heard the porch door slam, then Uncle Ray's hoarse voice. "Son of a bitch!" he cried. "That tree is comin' down!"

It was after one in the morning. I presumed he was bluffing, was having one of those irrational temper tantrums my father was also given to—flurries of profanity followed by over-enunciated declarations of preposterous solutions that will never come to pass. Growing up, my brother and I knew to dismiss dad's threats to shoot the dog if it "pissed on the floor one more goddamn time," his threats to throw out the television if we didn't "clean up our goddamn rooms," his threat to "turn the goddamn car around" and go back to Chicago when we were three miles outside of Phoenix.

"Annie!" Uncle Ray shouted. "Get the Blazer!"

Bluffing, I thought, rinsing my toothbrush.

Then I heard the jangling of keys. I stepped into the hallway, intercepted Annie. "What's going on?" I said.

"He's going to cut down the tree."

"But it's nearly two in the morning."

"I know," Annie said, wearily. "But he's crazy."

When doctor's orders convinced him to stop drinking, my great-grandfather supplanted his alcoholism for a lifetime of raising parakeets and gluing plastic Real Lemon containers atop the heads of his porcelain dog menagerie. A third cousin left home as a teenager to live with Liberace (my grandmother and her sisters insisted he was *only the pool boy*) and when Liberace died—leaving my cousin a nice chunk of change—he moved back to Chicago, rented a small apartment in a bad neighborhood and was picked up for trying to shoplift a package of liverwurst. To her dying day, my great aunt Virginia insisted she was born a twin, and that her twin was a gigantic sturgeon.

All this to say nothing of my genealogy research, to say nothing of the clinical depression and bipolar disorder common as pennies in relatives far less removed. To say nothing of "stress."

"Everyone in this family is crazy," I said, without irony, as I climbed into the Blazer's passenger seat. Annie stopped the truck a few feet from the tree's massive base, and Uncle Ray jumped out in a floppy camouflage hat with a chainsaw in one hand and a cigarette dangling from his mouth. He began to circle the tree. I tried not to think about the gasoline that powered both the saw in my uncle's hand and the truck in which I sat. Of this much I was certain: if my uncle exploded, if the car blew up, it would *not* be an act of God.

We watched, headlights trained on Uncle Ray, as though he was the principal artist in some absurd performance piece—illuminated, a finger of ash dangling precariously from the cigarette between his teeth, ducking bursts of embers, pressing saw to tree, springing back to purse it at his side.

Annie remembered then that she had a chain on the truck, a chain that, in winter, prevented the vehicle from sliding on slick gravel roads, but in weather conditions that were not inclement, merely kept the truck from going in reverse.

"Is that a problem?" I asked.

Annie unbuckled her seatbelt. "Only if the tree falls toward us."

For the first time in weeks, like a machine rebooting, my body whirred with energy. I sensed that we had passed "bad idea," were in "act of God" territory now. Annie's face was still, but her eyes darted quickly between the tree and her father. She didn't look frightened, just alert, tuned in, alive in a way that anticipated not gruesome endings, but bright ones. The look surprised me.

Uncle Ray tied a small branch to a length of yellow rope and lassoed it round the burning tree. I elbowed Annie. "He can't possibly pull it down himself."

Annie laughed, that laugh my Iowa family reserve for me and my mother, the *If Naïveté were a Religion, You'd be Jesus Christ* laugh. "No," Annie assured me. "*We're* going to pull it down."

She brought the truck closer, and Uncle Ray looped the rope around the Chevy Blazer's rusted front bumper.

"See," Annie said. "I knew we'd need to go in reverse."

I forced a laugh. *Killed by a burning tree,* I thought. *My mother will never forgive me.*

Annie patted my knee, "You can get out now if you want."

"No," I said. "I'm staying."

I thought of my father at my grandmother's, where no fires were raging, where the cupboards were stacked with canned goods and everyone was sound asleep, where they would all be alive in the morning, not part of a grisly forensics investigation.

"That don't sound like a good idea," my father would say when my brother and I wanted to slide down the staircase in a refrigerator box, melt Play-Doh in the microwave, or feed the dog Pop Rocks.

"Don't sound like a good idea," he'd say, chuffing cigarette smoke through his nose, a gentle dragon.

But he would have loved this—how the Blazer's motor roared, how the tree crackled and swooned beneath star formations unseen in Chicago. And the whirring I felt— that was him, too. Body buzzing with adrenaline, nervous system sparking, the physiology of chaos.

I looked at Annie. We were both smiling.

She pushed the car into reverse, slapped the wheel. "Here goes a miracle."

Wedding Town

My mother first saw my namesake in the OBGYN waiting room—a model in a bicentennial bikini smiling from the wrinkled, worn pages of a magazine.

"She was pretty," my mother told me. "Her name was Allison."

That was the entirety of the name origin story. Nothing terribly meaningful or symbolic—a pretty model had my name before I did. By the time I learned this, I was deep in my gawky adolescence, already realizing that "pretty" wasn't necessarily something a girl was, but rather something she did.

Bewildered, I watched as my girlfriends, who had once rescued half-dead robins, obsessed over the difference between Arabians and Clydesdales; who could quote whole pages of *Watership Down* and *Black Beauty,* became suddenly fixated on the distinction between gloss and matte, ivory and off-white, sheer and opaque. They could do "pretty," and while I sensed this was important, the urgency was lost on me. Pink or coral? Red or rust? Who cares? There were more pressing matters, like what the fuck are we going to do with the fetal squirrel that died in this shoebox?

Of course, my female friends' interest in color schemes, in powders, perfumes and nail polish had just about every-thing to do with boys. They wanted to be liked by boys, noticed by boys, but considering how the boys snapped our bras, leered at us, and catcalled, all I could think was, *They notice us too much.*

After ten years with Ben, the man I encouraged her to date, Megan decided to marry him and asked me to be the Maid-of-Honor. It was the first time I had been asked to participate in a wedding as anything more than a guest, and I was thrilled. While marriage inter-ests me neither in theory nor in praxis, I love weddings: the symbolism, the make-believe—veils, gowns, tuxe-dos, ornate cakes, and sonnets. To attend a wedding is to inhabit a place, *Wedding Town,* where everything is ordered, antiquated and simple: women handle the flow-ers, men handle the rings, everyone dances and toasts to love. Wedding Town is a living history museum where everyone has a part to play.

Generally, when I visited Wedding Town, it was as a mere ambassador from Homoville—I wore dark suits that made me look more like someone about to deliver a PowerPoint presentation on mutual funds than a guest at a friend's celebration. But Megan's wedding would be dif-ferent. As the maid-of-honor, I was practically the mayor of Wedding Town; I would stand beside the bride during the nuptials, maybe give a speech, wear a fancy dress. I was thirty that year and hadn't worn so much as a skirt in nearly a decade, and while the idea of a dress gave me pause, I understood the garment was symbolic, a marker of my role, *what one does in Wedding Town*. Liberace didn't wear bedazzled capes to bed; Justice Ginsberg doesn't wear her robe while trying on shoes. Rather, these articles of clothing are part of the act, part of the job—and I took my Maid-of-Honor job seriously.

As soon as I was old enough, I cast off the trappings of a feminine wardrobe, dismissing anything bright or whimsical in favor of blue jeans, shapeless pants, t-shirts, blazers, thrift-store pullovers, clunky boots, and oxfords. I owned such an abundance of black clothing that, upon viewing my closet space, Megan once asked, "Does Johnny Cash live here, too?"

"Soft butch," my gay friends called it—not masculine enough to be confused for a boy (though it had happened), but masculine enough to be pegged as a dyke. I preferred "androgynous," for the term felt less fixed, and I felt most at home in the gray area. My fashion sense (if one could call it that) had more to do with gender indifference than identity. I was not trying to "be male" or lure women with the broken laces on my Doc Martens, the thumbholes bored into the sleeves of my black hoodie. Instead, I was trying to escape the constraints of my first sixteen years—caged in taffeta skirts, choked by hairspray, pinched by pantyhose. I was done with that grotesque, pointless charade.

The first time someone mistook me for a boy, I was nineteen, visiting the local library in search of an obscure recording of Anne Sexton's rock band, *Her Kind*.

"Just a moment, young man," the librarian said.

I glanced around, but I was the only one there.

I followed her through the stacks, conversing about the dead poet, the lo-fi living room recording, Sexton's jam sessions with college kids, and the whole time the librarian referred to me as "sir." I let her, and it felt like some kind of victory. I was a Women's Studies minor, and I had transcended gender—ergo, I had won Women's Studies. After this, my college would have to open up a Women's Studies center and name it in my honor.

The librarian mis-gendered me right up until I presented her with my library card. She grew flushed then, bit her bottom lip, cleared her throat, but said nothing. She handed me my card, my Anne Sexton cassette tape, and told me to "have a nice afternoon."

I smiled. "You, too." I didn't need an apology because I wasn't offended. Despite what she'd called me, I was still every inch myself; I still had a vagina, and breasts, and still liked Anne Sexton. My identity didn't rely on pronouns or how they attached themselves to certain garments.

The night before the wedding, Megan, her soon-to-be-sister-in-law, Jill, and I stayed together in a suite at the riverside hotel where the ceremony and reception would take place. Complimentary amenities included a nightly delivery of warm chocolate chip cookies and cold milk in small glass jugs. Jill ate the cookies while Megan and I sat on the balcony, smoking cigarettes and drinking milk.

Reflecting on my role as matchmaker, I asked Megan what my finder's fee would be.

"Finder's fee," Megan scoffed. "Fuck your finder's fee in the face."

I stubbed out my cigarette. "Time for bed," I said. "Big day tomorrow, hooker."

We'd always spoken to each other this way. "Suck my dick" was a term of endearment. In college, we puzzled female peers who demonstrated their fondness for one another by way of hugs, pet names like "sweetie" and giggly declarations of "love ya!"

"Later, assface," Megan would yell across Campus Drive.

"Burn in hell," I'd shout back, middle fingers extended.

In the cafeteria, she'd call me a "fag" and I'd call her a "cocksucker," and many people mistook this for true hostility.

"You act like guys," a roommate once remarked.

But despite the coarse language, Megan was one of the few friends who, very early on, understood me, who took me on my own terms. A mutual friend once asked her if I was gay, and Megan shrugged and said, "She's Gruber."

With my bridesmaid dress hanging in the closet, my body full of milk and nicotine, Megan wished me a "good night, jackass," and I flicked out the light, excited for the day to come: the revelry, the role-playing, the free booze.

Inches from my face, the tiny, heavily perfumed woman hired to do our makeup introduced herself as "Erica, the makeup artist." Secretly, I took issue with her use of the term "artist." I realize it's a profession, but is there really anything artful about doing makeup for weddings? Can you really be creative, take any liberties? "Ah, I think we'll apply lipstick to your forehead and a splash of mascara to your lips—change it up!" For a Grace-Jones-themed wedding, maybe. A bubonic-plague-themed wedding, perhaps. But mostly you're doing the same thing over and over. Different shades, yes, but always the same color palette, always in the same places. There can be no innovation and, in my humble opinion, lack of innovation does not an artist make. Erica was no more a "makeup artist" than I, with my various adjunct teaching positions, was a "grammar artist."

However, rigid in my chair, draped in nothing but a hotel robe, Erica made me nervous; she had mastered something I'd never understood: femininity.

"How do you normally do your makeup?" Erica asked.

Normally, I didn't "do" any makeup; normally, I just wore skin. But there, before Erica, a woman who had built a career on gender norms, I felt uncomfortable admitting this. To admit to Erica that I didn't wear makeup felt on par with telling Oprah you never watched daytime television, or telling Mick Jagger you're "not into rock." So I opted for the most true and least awkward response, "Mostly just lip balm."

Erica-the-makeup-artist studied my face. With her manicured hands, she tilted my chin in several different directions before finally saying, "I'm going to airbrush you."

My only context for airbrushing was t-shirts printed with palm trees against hazy, apricot sunsets, "Steve & Laura Forever" foregrounded in swooning cursive.

I smiled politely, told her she could do whatever she deemed necessary.

She misted my face with foundation, glued false eyelashes onto my eyelids, smeared a thick coat of greasy lipstick across my mouth, then spun me around to face Jill and Megan.

They gasped. "Amazing."

"Your skin is amazing," "your eyes are amazing," "your mouth is amazing" (the latter compliment felt creepier than it did flattering). They kept firing the word at me but the pain of the first shot dulled with the fourth or fifth. What their flattery implied, however unintended, was that with the airbrushing, the slathering of cosmetics, I was improved.

Julie-the-hairdresser curled my short hair, lock by lock, into some version of a poorly constructed toupee. With my richly shadowed eyes, dark fanning lashes, all evidence of facial scars obliterated, I looked like the kind of woman I might consider hitting on before resolving she was probably straight. I was pretty and it made me polite. I didn't tell Julie that I hated my hair. Instead, I excused myself to the bathroom and proceeded to pull out the curls until they resembled something that had come organically from my head.

Though I used the term sparingly, "pretty" was part of my vernacular, and I employed it to describe things—orchids and cherry blossoms, certain jewelry, certain fabrics. Pretty made you nice, made others nicer to you.

If there is a truth all gender non-conforming women know, it is this: upon laying eyes on you, some men will automatically and inexplicably hate your ass. The priest who oversaw Megan's wedding was one such man. The previous day, standing before him in my baggy jeans, faded Grateful Dead t-shirt, with my boy-short hair, he looked vaguely disgusted when Megan introduced me as her Maid-of-Honor.

He shook my hand limply. "Father Corrigan."

During the rehearsal he chastised me for walking through imaginary chairs.

"You're walking through the chairs!" he barked, as though the following day, when the chairs were occupied by people, I would continue to barrel through them like some great, fumbling beast, tipping guests from their seats.

He chided me for being too slow to accept Megan's imaginary bouquet and for forgetting to give it back. "You must *return* the bouquet," he said, sneering.

Keeping hard eye contact with Father Corrigan, I thrust my fist full of invisible flowers toward Megan and told him that when I was actually clutching a bundle of flowers, I would remember that they did not belong to me.

Father Corrigan reminded me of the many pomade-slick, cigarette-reeking priests of my youth. The kind who wore gas station sunglasses, and paid too much attention to the pretty young mothers in the parish.

In the dressing room, I pulled on the nylons, snapped the lacy bra together and stepped into my dress: an ankle length halter, cut so low I had to ask Megan if there was a spare shawl laying around.

"A shawl?" Megan balked. "It's almost ninety degrees. What do you need a shawl for, grandma?"

I glanced down at my chest, and Megan rolled her eyes.

"Do you want something to cover your ankles, too?"

I crossed my arms. I wasn't opposed to my breasts—I just didn't want them on display, didn't want them rising from my dress like two loaves of raw dough.

Both my grandmothers had gigantic, pendulous breasts, and hated them. They complained that their breasts hurt their backs, limited clothing options, obstructed "pretty." In her seventies, my paternal grandmother got cancer and had a double mastectomy. My maternal grandmother suffered hers to her dying day. The way I saw it, breasts were for rearing children, attracting men, and tempting cancer.

I was all but flat-chested until I was twenty, when, suddenly, every pound I gained, I gained on my chest. In a year, I went from a small B-cup to a near-D. My friends noticed this, my mother noticed this, but worse, men noticed. I had inherited my grandmothers' breasts—a burden: two heavy, (to me) useless glands, two beacons of unwanted attention that I'd have to lug around for the rest of my life.

"I don't remember the dress being this revealing."

Megan sighed heavily. "Gruber, you're scandalized by v-neck sweaters. Take it easy, will you?"

Fiona, a British friend of mine and Megan's, had long ago taken to calling me "Constable." The afternoon of Megan's wedding, when Fiona came into the suite with gin-heavy gin & tonics for Megan, Jill, and me, she stepped back in shock.

"Constable?" she gasped in mock surprise. "Oh, you must be Allison today."

I took my drink and laughed, "Fuck off."

Few people call me by my given name. Over the years, I've been called names ranging from the tangentially understandable to the utterly inexplicable: Grubs, Chancellor, Professor Emeritus, Grubzilla, Scripto, Constable, and once, when Fiona was drunk, Colonel. ("You've been promoted," she slurred.)

Growing up, my father called me "Ace." This was a hybrid of my first and middle names—Allison Terese. Whether fishing, dancing in an Easter dress, or pouting over my broccoli, I was "Ace."

Today, however, I was Allison. Before she knew me, my mother named me after an idea, and the day of Megan's wedding, in my dress, my copious makeup, with my bronze shoes, and boobs on prominent display,

I was that idea—pretty, glamorous, enhanced—utterly feminine.

At the reception I danced with men. I danced with men not the way I used to in high school—The Junior High Zombie, bodies at an arm's length, rocking awkwardly from foot to foot, eyes wandering, searching for an excuse, an escape. This time I danced close. I danced sincerely. Dancing with men felt fine when it was a choice rather than an imperative.

I danced with Megan's father.

I danced with Megan's husband.

I danced with single men. Straight men.

When Megan approached me and said, "May I have this dance, motherfucker?" I danced with her, but found I missed dancing with men. The smell of cologne and perspiration, and the sturdiness of their bodies had triggered a kind of nostalgia.

My grandparents had always hosted New Year's Eve in their basement. It housed a full bar and a fireplace the adults would huddle around, smoking long, white cigarettes and drinking Manhattans, martinis, whiskey sours. At midnight, the kids were invited downstairs to dance with the grownups. My grandfather would play Bill Haley's "Rock Around the Clock" on the hi-fi and the children, high on sugar, overtired, would slide around, laughing themselves red in the face. Half-drunk by then, my father would hold out a meaty hand and ask, "You want to dance, Ace?"

I always did. He'd lift me and twirl me and swing my arms back and forth wildly as though preparing to fling me across the room.

"Now let me spin you," I'd say, and my father would crouch down, waddle under one of my skinny arms.

"You're a good dancer," he'd tell me, and I'd wiggle my hips, high on the feeling of transgression, on the inherent "pretend" of being girly; watched and watchable—to everyone in the room I felt irresistibly on display.

At Megan's reception I danced with abandon. Constable, Scripto, and Grubs feel self-conscious about dancing, would rather abstain, but apparently Allison loves to dance. Toward the end of the night, someone brought a drink out onto the dance floor and accidentally dropped it. Glass and ice skidded in all directions, but I was the only one to stop dancing. The spell had been broken.

On aching feet, I hobbled back to my hotel room, kicked my shoes off into my suitcase, threw my nylons in the trash, climbed eagerly out of my dress, and cursed as I peeled off the eyelashes, scarcely able to tell the real ones from the fake.

Scrubbed of makeup, free of the push-up bra, glasses on—I was myself again, no longer a resident of Wedding Town, returned to the world of ambiguity where people sometimes mistook me for a dude, where I didn't wear dresses or dance with men.

Later, when Megan asked me about the wedding, I said it was "nice."

"And?" Megan coaxed.

Figuring a compliment was what she was after, I mustered my best southern accent, "You looked real pur-ty."

"But did you have a good time?" Megan asked, impatiently.

"Yeah," I said. "It was fun, aside from the dress-ups."

Megan laughed. "Whatever, Tits McGee. You loved it."

A Lady Professor

Invariably, one slide in the carousel would be upside down. Sometimes, if it was a Pollock or Kandinsky, we couldn't immediately tell, but Professor Walker knew the difference and instantly employed a letter opener, key, box cutter or some other metal object to rattle the jam and free the upended slide. This always made me nervous. As a child, I was taught never to ram metal objects into electrically powered devices—no forks in the toaster, nails in the wall socket, box cutters in the slide carousel. I waited anxiously, in these moments, for Professor Walker to be electrocuted.

Students, mostly male, would offer to help. She was petite and attractive, and her frenetic energy sometimes gave her an air of helplessness. But she always refused assistance with her slides, swearing under her breath as she wrenched the small card from its slot.

"There," she'd sigh, blowing hair from her face once the odalisque or the Vitruvian Man had been unstuck.

The room was often dark, the only light emanating from the projector, the shadow of Professor Walker's wild hair whooshing across the screen as she dashed for her coffee or to consult her notes. When she paused, the room filled with the sound of pens whispering against paper, the mechanical whir of the machine—the most exquisite white noise.

There was no sentimentality in Professor Walker's discussion of art—just dates, locations, and compositional observations with lyrical names like "emuleta," "pieta," "chiaroscuro." Her British accent gave the foreign words an added exoticism.

I was eighteen. Prior to Intro to Art History, my vocabulary for art had been limited to "pretty," "weird," and "wow." At the start of each class period, Professor Walker would have us write short responses to whatever painting or sculpture was projected on the screen. These were considered exams, for which I often borrowed phrases I'd heard Professor Walker use: "Highly stylized," "A tonal juxtaposition," "Grandiose gesture."

"Well done!" she'd write above my responses. "Solid critique!" The lukewarm compliments were rendered significant by exclamation points.

Professor Walker's accent, the dramatic lighting, the language, and my consistently high examination scores made the class my favorite. I couldn't wait until the semester was over so I could take my A in Art History to the Art Institute of Chicago where I would stand before a Rembrandt or a Warhol and discuss it, "solidly," at length.

Maybe, I thought, *I should change my major . . .*

Pride, of course, comes before the fall.

One morning, Duchamp's *Fountain* was projected at the front of the room. I knew the piece, I knew the story behind it—a toilet from a tavern in an art museum—and so I sat down with my pen, my blue book, and began my critique. "Surrealist," I wrote. "Classic surrealist. It pushes against what is socially acceptable, exposes basic human behaviors..."

A week later, I received my graded exam. Across the top, Professor Walker had written, "Solid discussion of Surrealism, but this is Dada." Then, dangling like some dark token in the lower left hand corner of my essay, an angular F—accompanied by the phrase, "A pity!"

I was embarrassed by my mistake and accepted my grade. And I was in awe of that final phrase—it was so precise, so flippant, so merciless: "A pity!"

Exclamation point.

End of discussion.

College gave me a very specific idea about academia. Rather than twisting in an office chair, waiting for death or a pension, one could spend one's life waxing philosophical about Disney films with Fulbright scholars, and soaking up the adoration of moony students who raced to the registrar to ensure a spot in your course on Medieval Hybrid Poetics.

Adjunct professor—it sounded like a beginning, a way in. I did not yet understand that an adjunct is—by definition—an addition to a pre-existing thing, but not an essential part of it. Like toilet seat covers or green food coloring in beer.

While my alma mater had infused me with aspirations of Virginia Woolf-ian proportions, I wound up a Wile E. Coyote, repeatedly pummeled by the anvils of poverty and disillusionment. I had to take whatever classes I could get.

Teach a course on public speaking?

Why, yes, that would be most agreeable.

Intro to Religious Studies?

I used to go to church, why the hell not?

A class exploring all the cultures of Latin America?

Por supuesto!

The first class I was offered was a section of *The Legacy Sequence:* a pair of courses all freshmen were required to take. And because it was a requirement, all students despised *The Legacy Sequence.*

Upon hiring me, my department head, Dr. Brown, acknowledged this sentiment, "Most students feel... uh, somewhat... resentful. And this resentment often presents *Legacy* instructors with a unique—how shall I say?—challenge."

Inexperienced and desperate, I enthusiastically assured Dr. Brown I was up to the challenge.

The first semester I taught what was known as *Western Legacy,* a course in which students read Plato, Homer, Aristotle, Shakespeare, and Thomas Jefferson. Full-time faculty were at liberty to express umbrage at the fact the *Legacy* reading list was devoid of women or people-of-color, but being a lowly adjunct, I gathered up my feminism, my multiculturalism and stuffed them into a coin purse.

The week before the start of classes, I attended a mandatory orientation for part-time faculty new to teaching *Western Legacy.* The orientation was led by a ruddy-faced, elderly full-timer who had a strong affinity for Goethe and gin. He began his lecture on ancient Greek culture by saying, "In the good old days, men were in control of three things: language, currency, and women."

When a few people chuckled, I became acutely aware of the fact that I was the only woman in the room. Not wanting to appear overly sensitive, I looked down at my yellow legal pad, smiled and let out a half-hearted "heh." *Hey, guys, I'm down with misogyny, so long as it's highbrow.* I was certain this was nothing more than some obsolete, over-educated buffoon's attempt at humor, but it felt as if he'd said, "In the good old days, men controlled language, currency, and women weren't *Western Legacy* instructors."

Fortunately, that first semester, I was given a wonderful group of students. They called me "professor." They were punctual, attentive, and polite. I even managed to sneak some Woolf and de Beauvoir onto the syllabus under the asterisk "tentative."

One afternoon, while grading in the windowless hovel shared by the *Legacy* adjuncts, where mice stole teabags and delivery trucks spilled their exhaust, Dr. Brown paid me an unexpected visit. He informed me that the *Legacy* Department had hired a Thomas Jefferson impersonator who would be visiting campus the following Monday. This struck me as a pathetic allocation of department funds. What's more, when I considered my meager wages, it felt downright insulting. (Back then, I would have donned a powdered wig and recited *The Declaration of Independence* for a pack of Camel Lights.)

"Cool," I said.

Dr. Brown agreed that it was cool, but explained that full-time *Legacy* faculty did not share our enthusiasm. Full-time faculty balked when Dr. Brown suggested the Thomas Jefferson impersonator visit their classrooms.

"Now I have this Thomas Jefferson impersonator," Dr. Brown lamented, "and nowhere for him to go."

I nodded soberly. "That is really unfortunate."

Dr. Brown agreed that it was unfortunate and told me that, in light of the circumstances, he would bring the displaced Thomas Jefferson impersonator to my classroom on Monday.

The impersonator was pretty much what one might expect—middle-aged, Virginian accent, bespectacled, bewigged, wielding the sort of folk art cane one might find in a gift shop at Monticello. I was fresh out of art school and the sort of performance art I was accustomed to involved women gnawing on life-sized wax farm animals, so I found the literalness—the benign branch of performance art that was dead president mimicry—particularly absurd.

When Dr. Brown introduced me to Fake Thomas Jefferson, I expected the impersonator to shake my hand and say, "Hey. How's it goin'? I'm Dave." Instead, he folded into a courtly bow, put a hand to his chest and in charmed disbelief gasped, "A lady professor?"

I was mortified. I've always loathed the word "lady," connoting, as it does, parasols, fainting couches, and Tom Jones.

"Yes," I demurred. "That's the one."

"Why, in Virginia," declared Thomas Jefferson, "we do not have lady professors at university."

Dr. Brown was visibly pleased by the authenticity of the performance, but I was panicked, convinced that the rapport I spent all semester building with my freshmen would, in minutes, be undone at the hands of a Thomas Jefferson simulacrum.

How could my students respect a "lady"? No one wants to learn from a "lady." No one ever says, "I would like a lady surgeon." No one ever dreams of having a "lady president," or hopes their plane is flown by a "lady pilot." We don't use the word "lady" to refer to women in positions of power or authority. The word is derisive, anything but empowering. Like an adjunct, a lady is a non-essential thing.

I smiled tightly and took my seat, flustered by what I told myself was basically a high-brow clown.

My students somehow managed to remain awake and engaged as Thomas Jefferson roamed the classroom, tapping his cane and reminiscing about The Revolution, his pal John Adams, the penning of *The Declaration,* and the small matter of slaves.

After forty-five minutes of patriotic blathering, the impersonator brought his charade to a close. Part of me hoped for a question-and-answer session where my students might show Dr. Brown all they had learned in my class—dazzle him with some critical thinking, reference Plato, quote Shakespeare.

Instead, Thomas Jefferson rebounded, pivoted on his cane and earnestly inquired, "In the course of this term, which texts have you encountered?"

Please, I thought, *don't say anything about "The Second Sex."*

But there was no response. My students sat silently, gaping at one another, baffled.

Once more, Thomas Jefferson queried them, "I say, what texts, young men and gentlewomen, has your kindly lady professor been teaching you this term?"

I cringed, both at his use of the word "lady" and my students' inability to answer the simple question. When Dr. Brown glanced at me, puzzled by their silence, my face began to burn. I didn't know what was happening. Had the mere suggestion of my lady-ness caused them to forget I had taught them anything at all?

Finally, the student sitting next to me raised his hand shyly. Rather than addressing Thomas Jefferson, he turned to me, "Professor, when he says 'texts' does he mean books?"

I was sure that Fake Thomas Jefferson had ruined my chances of being offered another course at my alma mater, and some nights, I indulged revenge fantasies: *You'll be impersonating Grover Cleveland in hell, you one-trick son of a bitch.*

But they kept me.

"The Latin American flavor? Or the Asian flavor?" Dr. Brown asked.

Never mind that I have always despised figurative use of the word "flavor," I wasn't remotely qualified to teach either section of *Global Legacy.*

Tentatively, I voiced my concerns, "Dr. Brown, my background is in—"

He waved dismissively, "Just pick one."

So I chose Latin America because I had taken two semesters of Spanish twelve years ago, because I liked Pablo Neruda, and because I had once been to Cancun on spring break. It was a bit like deciding I could teach quantum physics because I was familiar with the concept of numbers.

The January between fall and spring semester, I spent a great deal of time trying to educate myself on all of Latin America's history, culture, and literature. That month, I also wiled away many hours contemplating the word "fraud."

Fortunately, as it was for *Western Legacy,* the curriculum for *Legacy: Latin America* was largely preordained. The department chose the texts; I simply had to teach them. We read about the horrors of Columbus and Hernán Cortés, we explored the activism of Rigoberta Menchú, and analyzed the paintings of Diego Rivera and Frida Kahlo.

Rather, I *alone* read and considered these things; this group of freshmen was demonstratively disinterested. As a punitive measure, I began to give simple reading quizzes that they flagrantly failed. To the question, "From what country was Rigoberta Menchú?" I received answers like, "South America." To the question, "Who was Hernán Cortés?" I fielded insights such as, "He was the first Latin American to express his feelings."

There was no Che Guevera impersonator on hand to witness the disaster that was my section of *Legacy: Latin America*; to witness how I often grew short tempered and, at the slightest provocation, kicked students out of class; to see how the evictee—or evictees—would gather their things while mumbling, "Ay caramba" or "Dios mío," inciting a chorus of laughter among their remaining peers; to hear me yell that if I heard one more remark about Frida Kahlo's facial hair, I was seriously going to lose my shit. Part of the problem with *Global Legacy* was that I hadn't, myself, mastered the material. Once, while a blank map of Latin America was projected against the white board, a student, who had a strong interest in drug cartels, asked me which part was Colombia.

I froze.

Not unlike many fellow Americans, my geography is abysmal. I stared at the map, considered lying to them, tracing a random shape and declaring, "This one."

I also considered admitting that I did not know, but with this particular group, any admission of ignorance was an open invitation to idiocy: references to the Taco Bell dog, Pepe Gonzales, *Scarface*.

"You know," I said, "no one really knows for sure. The location of Colombia remains a mystery."

Because I had been so unforgiving with this group, because they had forced me to play, "bad cop," they didn't know whether or not to laugh. For a fleeting moment, I felt guilty, felt I'd been too hard on them. *Poor kids, they don't know if it's safe to laugh. I am the Joan Crawford of* Global Legacy.

"I'm kidding," I said.

And when they laughed, it was eerily obligatory.

Of course, I could have gone to Dr. Brown for advice, could have told him my students were uncooperative, immature, out-of-control little shits. *I've tried everything,* I could have told him, *and nothing works.* But after some deliberation, I realized I didn't want to ask for help; unless she establishes herself as independent—as Mary Poppins, Professor Walker—students will assume a female teacher is malleable, soft, a lady. I had to have their respect.

By then, I had worked with an adjunct math instructor whose students routinely made her cry—race-out-of-the-room-arm-flung-over-her-brow-cry. Other instructors, mostly women, would rush to coddle her, console her, and send her back into the classroom.

"They just don't listen to me," this instructor complained, dabbing at her eyes.

I never participated in the comfort sessions, thinking, *Maybe they don't listen to you because they can't make out your words over the sound of your sobbing.* The math adjunct was the embodiment of what I never wanted to be; it was one thing to get angry, frustrated, and it was quite another to cry.

Ladies withered in the face of adversity. *Ladies* cried.

While contending with *Global Legacy*, I added another college to my growing list of employers, a small institution that primarily served working adults, mostly new immigrants. I was to teach a straightforward composition course that met on Wednesday nights.

Composition courses were easy, but boring. Composition was "writing for people who do not wish to write." Comp—as my writer friends called it—was where MFA's went to die; a graveyard of dreams whose tombstones read like angry cover letters: *the market is oversaturated with degrees in the humanities, colleges are adopting corporate models, and no one values literature.*

Composition classes were all about intro, body, and conclusion. No Socrates or Flaubert, no space on the curriculum for a little bit of Modernist Poetry or concepts any more complex than Ethos, Pathos, and Logos.

But my Midwestern upbringing had furnished me with a strong work ethic—I had a job to do, damnit. I tried to think of the objectives as a sworn oath, "To serve and protect grammar, syntax, and MLA citation."

The new class had only four students on the roster, and on the first day, as I stood before them, tediously reviewing the syllabus, a fifth student entered the room. Her makeup was clownish. Though thin, her clothes were too tight and cut into the soft flesh of her arms and thighs.

Irritated by the interruption, I thrust a syllabus in her direction and told her she wasn't on my roster.

"My name's Kim," she said. "I just got added."

Her face was as lined and hollowed as a late November pumpkin. She was missing teeth. The other women in the class stared curiously at Kim, and as I watched them purposefully establish physical distance from her, I wondered if I had accidentally let in a transient.

Back then, I began semesters by asking students to go around the room and state what they hoped to get out of the course. I should have known to stop this practice after using it with my *Global Legacy* class where the answers included, "credit," "a passing grade," and "nada."

Alas, that evening, though the answers were stock and simple, they were without sarcasm. Altagracia wanted to improve her written English; Kenya liked to write, but only poetry; Maria hoped to get a better job, and Lourdes was honest, "They told me I had to take this class."

When it was Kim's turn to answer the question, she explained that she'd recently been released from prison. After this admission, the other students nodded empathetically, but squirmed and turned red.

"Don't worry," Kim said. "I didn't kill anybody; I was just a hooker."

Kim never did fully assimilate into our small class. For one, she regularly said things that made me, and the other women, incredibly uncomfortable. But while my students had the luxury of shifting in their seats and blushing, as the teacher, I had to field comments like, "Chlamydia sucks, trust me" and "Never buy coke from a Filipino," as though they were as commonplace as malapropisms.

Among a myriad of academic problems, Kim was chronically late to class. There was always some crisis— the guy who was supposed to drive her to school never showed up; she didn't have bus fare; she had to meet her parole officer; she had to visit her son in foster care; she took a nap and overslept.

Though tardiness was a major pet peeve, one that I never let my *Global Legacy* students get away with, what could I possibly say to Kim, a forty-year-old woman—or was she fifty?—that would be any more foreboding, any more threatening or humiliating than what she had already heard as a junkie, a prostitute, an inmate at the Cook County Correctional Facility?

"You're in danger of failing the course," I told Kim one evening during break. She'd been late and had missed my talk on "dependent and independent clauses." Distressed, Kim put her hands over her face. Hers were large hands—bloated, purplish-red. Years later, I would learn that such hands are symptomatic of long-term heroin use.

"Sorry," she said, faintly.

"You must make a concerted effort to arrive on time to class."

Kim slumped over her desk, buried her head in her arms and began swearing. I knew I could walk away from her despair and it wouldn't even rank among the coldest things a person had ever done to her. I crouched down beside the desk, touched one of her shoulders. "Are you all right?"

She lifted her head. "Fuck no."

Then Kim did the one thing I had anticipated as an eventuality in my teaching career: she started to cry.

I panicked. "Let's talk after class," I said. "Maybe we can figure something out."

But Kim assured me I was not the reason for her distress. "I was robbed last night," she said. "Someone came into my apartment and smashed up all my shit."

I asked her if she'd called the police, and she shook her head, wiped her tears and leaned in so close I could smell aluminum and old tobacco on her breath, "It was my pimp."

I stood quickly, grabbed at the back of my neck, "Well, how does your pimp know where you live?"

She looked up at me, open-mouthed, and said nothing. I was, allegedly, a "master of the fine arts," but I wasn't Prospero. In the stark light of Kim's life, literature felt as dubious as magic.

Some professors I knew, women mostly, were exceedingly warm with their students, counseling them, embracing them, creating a network of paper extensions around their personal crises. These women seemed more determined to achieve martyrdom than tenure track.

A middle-aged instructor at one of my schools routinely called her students "hon."

"I'll go grab you another copy of the syllabus, hon," she'd say, like a waitress serving up second helpings of curriculum. *Hon*-colleague would have likely found a crisis hotline for Kim to call, but not before giving her a big hug and assuring her that everything was going to be all right.

And though I could be kind, I was not warm, so once more I touched Kim's shoulder, and gave her the truth: "I don't know what to tell you."

Modeled after NPR's "This, I Believe" series, I had the women write a two-page, double-spaced essay explaining—with proper grammar, sentence structure and syntax—a conviction they strongly held. "This, I Believe" was the first and last assignment Kim submitted. Instead of two double-spaced pages, Kim wrote four-and-a-half, single-spaced, Comic Sans.

Contrary to my expectation, her essay was not about drugs, nor was it about prostitution or jail time, and began simply, "I believe I want my son back." Of course, the essay stumbled into ruminations about what it might be like to live in Tokyo; polemics against Mayor Daley; musings on food additives; meditations on a golden retriever, a backyard, a brother who played little league, a mother who was always making sandwiches and a father who only wore suits—idyllic recollections so vivid and peculiar it was impossible to discern whether she was recalling her own childhood or imagining a perfect one.

Had this been a creative writing course, I would have marveled at the courage and invention—the effortless glide from one unrelated thought to the next, the miraculous syntheses. Artists from James Joyce to Allen Ginsberg had been lauded for as much.

But this was comp, where precision was key. Adherence to rules: does the introduction communicate the main point? Do all paragraphs begin with topic sentences that tie back to the main point? Does the conclusion restate the main point? Is there a point?

A pity!

The essay broke my heart. There was no neat meaning, but the themes were sharp and wholly comprehensible—tremendous longing, total desperation. Kim ended the essay abruptly, "This, I believe, every little boy deserves a puppy."

Bound by the rubric, I had no choice but to assign the paper an "F." I scribbled a note at the bottom, "Kim, please see me. Opportunity to revise . . ."

*   *   *

Kim never returned to pick up her paper. Two weeks passed before I went to see her advisor who nonchalantly informed me that Kim was back in prison on a parole violation.

"What happened?" I asked.

Her advisor raised her eyebrows and shrugged. "Drugs? Thievery? Hooking? Take your pick."

I cleared my throat. "Will she get out?"

Again, her advisor shrugged.

"That's too bad," I said. "She was a nice person."

Her advisor smirked. "No," she replied coolly. "She really wasn't."

Typically, I disposed of uncollected papers, but I held on to Kim's. Sometimes I re-read the essay and regretted dooming it with an "F," as though a "D" would have somehow kept her from prison.

One evening, noticing her absence, Lourdes pointed to the desk where Kim used to sit. "What happened to that lady?"

Coming from Lourdes, "lady" didn't sound pejorative. Rather, it sounded reverent, respectful, like a bowed utterance of "sir" or "ma'am," an admission of "you belong here, with us." I heard warmth in the word, as if a heart beat inside it. Knowing Kim's fate, I felt my throat close. I shrugged.

"Is she coming back?" Lourdes asked.

"No," I said, on second thought adding, "which is a shame, because she was a good writer."

Lourdes squinted in disbelief. The other women looked up, puzzled, but too polite to question the validity of what I was saying. I was, after all, the professor—adjunct or not. Surely I knew a good writer from a poor one.

"She *was* a good writer," I repeated, somewhat insistently, trying to counter their collective surprise, trying to ensure that that "lady" left our classroom not as a pathetic, worthless figure, but as a mystery with qualities unknown.

Student Fiction

Dr. L laid a diagram on the table: a sketch of the female human body. The transparent flesh, the stark skeletal structure, the beaded webs of the lymphatic system, the dense map of the vascular system. She circled the left nipple and the cluster of lymph nodes that pearled in the drawing's armpit.

"My plan is to take the nipple," she explained, "and all these lymph nodes, and the cancer, of course."

"Of course." I blinked and stared at the drawing, her circles. Everything looked simpler on paper—more literal, and in this way, utterly misleading. I was skeptical of road maps because the terrain they depict is never really the terrain you traverse.

"Tell me what you're thinking," said Dr. L.

Dr. L was kind. Not much older than me, maybe even a year or two younger. Perhaps because of this, she spoke to me as a peer rather than a slow-witted dog, as other doctors had. I ran my hands through my hair, leaned back and exhaled.

"I'm thinking . . ."

I was thinking of the Civil War doctors who chloroformed amputees before taking their limbs. I was thinking how for more minor procedures, like extracting bullets from the chest cavity or setting broken bones, patients got grain alcohol and a stick between the teeth. I was thinking how they must have screamed, and how cathartic such screams must have been. I was thinking what a pity modern medicine, so tidy and polite, leaves no room for shrieking.

I touched the diagram between us, made a joke. "I'm thinking this woman looks nothing like me."

When I was sixteen, I had to dissect a frog in Biology class. This was not traumatic for me. In fact, I looked forward to the exercise. It felt like a rite of passage to dissect a frog in Biology class, as American as the Pledge of Allegiance.

For the dissection, the teacher had the class work in pairs, and I was paired with Missy. Missy had adorably curly hair that bounced in dark ringlets around her broad, cherubic face. Missy was on the cheerleading squad, she was dating a varsity quarterback. Missy is the girl who gets killed first in horror movies. Missy is a stock character, a cliché, but she was absolutely real.

Missy did not want to dissect the frog. She was adamantly, petulantly opposed to the dissection. She half-heartedly started a petition to ban the practice altogether that I suspected was less about ethics than a certain squeamishness.

The frog was not the first dead animal I had seen. On many occasions, I'd watched my uncle kneel beside a deer carcass, open the buck from throat to cock, reach in and pull out shapeless hunks of blood-slick organs. Then there were the pet hamsters whose small, stiff corpses I'd plucked from their cage. By the time I was a teenager I could bait a hook, could grasp a writhing carp and wrench the wire from its bloodied, gasping mouth and feel no more moved than if I was buttering bread.

Sensing my indifference, Missy slid the scalpel in my direction. I flipped the frog on its back. The air in the room smelled strange—chemical, yet earthy. Unfamiliar with the smell of formaldehyde, I presumed this was the natural scent of many dead amphibians. As I slit the smooth, white belly open with the scalpel's tip, Missy gasped in horror. "How can you do that? I mean, how can you *do* that?"

I shrugged, kept going. "Just a frog."

She spun away dramatically, curls bobbing, and buried her face in her hands. "I can't look," she squealed. "I just can't look."

I couldn't wait to see what was inside the frog. We had been shown diagrams—here, the kidneys; here, the bladder; here, the heart. But I knew the depictions would be nothing like the real thing, just some gross approximation, like sex in movies. The reality, I figured, must be much more astonishing.

Later, to my friends, I made ruthless fun of Missy, gave my best impression of an uptight southern belle: "Good heavens! I do not buhlieve what you are doin' to that poor creatchuh!"

"The way she was acting," I told my friends, "you'd think I was filleting a live kitten."

I hadn't been squeamish; I hadn't felt anything. But watching Missy's reaction had made me uncomfortable—like I was incapable of comprehending some basic truth about life and death.

Two weeks after the dissection, Missy died in a car accident while making a left-hand turn on a two-lane road. Given Missy's popularity, the whole school attended her wake like a homecoming game. Just as weeks earlier we'd stood outside the Metro to see the Violent Femmes on a school night—giddy with disobedience, passing clove cigarettes, singing softly, *I hope you know/this will go down/ on your permanent record*—we now waited in line outside the funeral home to see Missy. We weren't smoking. We weren't barking out teenage anthems with apathetic abandon. Inside the parlor, I encountered a smell similar to that I attributed to the frogs and wondered if it was a trick of memory. I had never seen a dead body before.

They look like they're asleep, I'd heard adults say of the dead. But this is a trope. The stillness of a corpse is nothing like that of a living being in repose. A cadaver is no more like a sleeping human than a stone is like a toad.

Missy's body had been badly damaged in the accident, and in the coffin, despite the mortuary's readjustments and thick makeup, her brow jutted slightly, giving her classic feminine beauty a mannish, Cro-Magnon quality. I watched others pause to kneel before the coffin, but when I glimpsed Missy's body nestled in the casket's satin, I felt weak-kneed, a rushing in my ears, and walked past quickly without offering a prayer.

When I arrived home that night, my father greeted me at the door. "How'd it go?" he asked, awkwardly.

And then, for the first and last time in my life, I fell against his body and wept.

My parents were to pick me up and drive me to the hospital. I told myself it was kind of like when, as a pre-teen, they'd take me to the mall. Only instead of meeting friends to drink Orange Julius, ride the escalators, and shoplift dollar eye shadows, I was going to meet doctors, nurses, and have a portion of my left breast removed.

I made coffee, and then remembered I couldn't drink it. As I poured the pot down the drain, I thought about how my students described death in their fiction. Some character was always gnashing his teeth, punching walls, dropping the phone. Some character always cried out to god, screamed, or tore at her hair while crashing to her knees. Death, in their stories, was a collage of incredible gestures. *In a hospital?* I'd ask a student during workshop. *Do you think one would actually do that in a hospital?* The student almost always conceded that, no, one probably wouldn't fall bellowing to the ground at the bedside of a loved one—at least not in the quiet sterility of a hospital room. *Wouldn't that be amazing,* I thought that morning, watching the last of my fair-trade French roast swirl away.

In the weeks since my diagnosis, I had come to believe that death was about as dramatic and dignified as slipping on a banana peel at the edge of the Grand Canyon: you're caught off guard, you flail for a while, and you're gone.

An "active metaphor," I thought, remembering there were types.

"Types?" a poet friend once asked. She was, on some levels, a fraud, but she was beautiful and I was a little in love with her so I paid her fraudulence no mind.

"Yes," I smiled. "Mixed, Root, Submerged . . . "

This was the year when all the poets I knew were writing abstract verse about birds. I was no better, filling my fiction with sea life of the most rote variety—carp, goldfish—nothing exotic, only the dullest, most common kinds for me. I preferred my work straightforward and subdued. I never bothered much with metaphors implicit, submerged, or—as in the case of my poet friend—wholly incomprehensible.

In the hospital room I sat on the edge of the bed, self-consciously rubbing my hands along my unshaven legs. Had I known I was about to get cancer, about to sit in a knee length gown in front of my parents, I would have invested in a pack of Daisy razors.

My interior life was suddenly visible to my parents. Until now they'd only had a rough idea—lives in Milwaukee, teaches English, single, enjoys reading. Now they were exposed to the guts—bookshelves flanked by *Lesbian Readings of Virginia Woolf* and the greatest hits of the Marquis de Sade. In her refrigerator nothing but Tabasco sauce, an expired container of cottage cheese, and a half-drunk bottle of cheap chardonnay. She doesn't mate her socks or make her bed, and she definitely doesn't shave her legs.

A nurse entered the room and asked me which breast was being operated on. When I was a kid, I'd had a number of successive surgeries on my left leg, so knew this question was the surgical equivalent of "taxiing for takeoff."

"Left," I confirmed.

She checked something off on her clipboard and winked. "Good! That's what we've got ya down for."

My mother and I shared a forced smile. I wanted to say something, to crack a joke about my situation, but before I could speak, my ride had arrived. Stepping up onto the frame, I wondered if the gurneys used to take people to surgery were the same ones that delivered them to the morgue. If you died in surgery, did they just whip a sheet over your head and whisk you down to the freezers? Did anyone ever die from breast surgery? I knew St. Agatha had had hers lopped off and survived, but then, she was aided by an angel.

When a nurse asked me to give my glasses to my mother, I asked why.

"You won't need them," she explained sweetly. "Mom can hang onto them for safekeeping."

I felt incredulous. I was thirty-four years old. I had paid for those frames, those lenses, not my mother. But what really rattled me was how easily she had said, "You won't need them." I always needed my glasses. Without my glasses, the journey from the bedroom to the bathroom was perilous. Without my glasses, I couldn't identify my face in the mirror. I shook my head.

"Just let me hang onto them for a little bit," my mother gently urged.

"No," I said. "No one is taking my glasses."

Then I started to cry. "You. Can't. Take. My. Glasses."

"Allison," my mother said, embarrassed by my outburst.

"I won't even do this," I cried, slapping my free arm against the side of the gurney. "I won't even have this surgery if I can't have my glasses."

"What's the difference if Allison keeps her glasses?" my father said.

"She doesn't need them," my mother snapped. "They want her to leave them here. There must be a reason for that—"

"Yeah," my father said, "but what if she just hung onto 'em until she got to the operating room—"

"I couldn't even have my coffee this morning," I wailed.

My mother's cheeks were flushed; she and the nurse exchanged looks.

"You can keep your glasses on," the nurse said.

I quieted then, stunned by my victory.

"I can?"

In a season of losses, it was a small victory, but a victory nonetheless. Quelled by vindication and Valium, I wiped my eyes with the back of my hand. "If anyone takes them off, they better be back on me when I wake up."

My father trudged back to his post at the window, my mother rolled her eyes, chewed her bottom lip and the nurse squeezed her shoulder.

"She's just nervous," the nurse explained.

But I wasn't "just nervous," I was ridiculous, a character in a student's story.

Some kids at our high school made a memorial site for Missy, adorning the light pole her car had skidded into with carnations, ribbons, and black and white Xerox copies of her face. For weeks afterwards, when passing that intersection you would see teenagers twirling crepe paper, laying flowers, collecting glass. Days after the accident, glass from the car windows still glittered in the sidewalk and the road. People said some shards were dimmed by blood. My friends and I crouched along the road, depositing our findings into envelopes. This wasn't about mourning Missy; this was about wanting a souvenir from the gift shop of sudden demise. This was about trying to fathom how death could actually happen, could ever be anything more than an abstraction; like love, marriage, and adulthood itself.

I felt like a thief and slid my envelope, full of windshield glass, into an old Bible—trying, at least, to give my spoils a holy hiding place. Sometimes, I'd tug the envelope from its pages and peer inside, try to imagine the moment she died. What was she thinking? Was there music playing? If so, was it something good like My Bloody Valentine or something dumb like Color Me Badd? Did she know it was over? Did it feel like something violent or something soft?

On the outskirts of the football field, a friend and I shared a Marlboro light while swapping rumors about the accident.

"She died on impact," my friend said.

I took the cigarette. "What does that mean?"

"Right away," she said. "Like, instantly."

I didn't like this idea. There had to be a moment before, a space, even if only a split second. That afternoon our English teacher, Mr. Lee, described a metaphor as the absence of "like" or "as."

"A simile is approximate," he said. "A metaphor is exact. There is no gap between the object and its metaphor— they are one and the same."

That night, I took the envelope out and pressed the pads of my fingers into the bottom crease, sprinkled shallowly with glass. I did it again the next night, and a few more after that. Sometimes the contents of that envelope felt historical, like a bit of sand from the beaches of Normandy, a clump of earth from Gettysburg. Sometimes, though, the contents seemed grim and meaningless—the remnants of an instantly fatal car accident.

Warm under heavy blankets, I woke in the recovery room with my glasses on.

"Is it over, or am I dreaming?" I asked the woman checking my vitals. The question was not rhetorical.

"All done," she replied, brightly.

My insides hadn't yet woken from the anesthesia, and because of this, though hungry, I could not eat. I imagined wresting myself from my body and into a can or jar—just my brain, my thoughts. I could be preserved like creamed corn, strawberry jelly, pimento-stuffed olives—things with a long shelf life, things that, in that moment, I'd kill to eat. I'd be okay then; simplified. I wouldn't feel the bandages around my chest, the prickling pain of nerve endings fumbling for one another in the dark of my body. I buzzed the nurses' station.

"Can I get up?" I asked the nurse as she entered the room.

"You want to?" She sounded surprised.

"Yeah," I said. "I do."

For an hour, I walked around the square of the ward, pulling my IV along like a tall dog on wheels. All the patient rooms were dark but for the occasional television flickering bruised hues. Each time I passed them, the nurses at the station smiled. Sometimes, they waived encouragingly, like sideliners at a marathon. My intention was to walk until morning, to see the sunrise, to make the nurses dizzy with my laps, because I was not sick.

In the movies, in my students' fiction, cancer is obvious. Someone is coughing blood, someone looks clammy, or pale, or green, or is fainting all the time, or is looking pale and clammy while fainting. Doing laps around the oncology ward, I made my students' fiction a sort of diagnostic tool—my color was not off, I was not sweating profusely or passing out; there was no blood seeping from any orifice where blood ought not seep. I was nothing like the characters that died in their stories.

I did not like where I had been: I didn't like the eternity I'd slipped into when asleep in the operating room.

Like a patient etherized on a table . . . .

Think about that, I'd tell my students when we read Eliot. *That's not asleep. That's not "at rest." That's about as close to dead as we get while we're still alive.*

But this was still only a simile, an approximation. I kept walking the ward, numbly at times, at times shuddering, until exhaustion crashed through me like a ghost. Defeated, I returned to my room, struggled back into bed, and with my glasses on, let sleep, real sleep, have its way.

They said Missy died on impact; one moment she was driving, the next she was oblivion. *There was no in between,* I told myself. *She just ended.* And maybe this was true. Maybe, for Missy, there was no "in between." Maybe there is no distinct boundary between alive and dead. Maybe the difference is nothing more than the transition between a red light and a green light.

But most of us prefer to deal in similes, where there is a border. Contrary to my students' fiction, this is how the border is traversed:

You shower and brush your teeth. You drink your coffee: the overpriced organic French roast. You drive your shitty car to the hospital and park in the underground garage. You place your breast in a vice and suffer the inquisitions of a quiet, gray haired man who will finally clap his cold hand on your shoulder and say, "This is going to be cancer."

You don't cry. You don't vomit. You stare for a while, then you take a Xanax, and once in your shitty car, you apply deodorant because you have to go to work. When class is over, you scrape frost off your windshield and drive home. Once there, you sit dead-eyed in front of the television, and wonder how you're going to tell your mother you have cancer. Then you think of the absurd: how cancer will allow you to tell your mother you are gay, how you want Megadeth played at your funeral.

But at some point the cold facts are too much to bear, so you conjure up the metaphors, the tropes. Death is slipping on a banana peel because the moment between slipping and falling is the most protracted part, the part where you are most ridiculous and wild—and it's true, you are. And maybe you're mixing your metaphors, perhaps you're indulging in clichés, but that long second between sliding off the peel and the impact is not a border, or a likeness; it's pure life.

Nurse Navigator settled into the chair beside my bed, smiled. "Whenever you're ready."

I glanced sidelong at her, sighed. I wanted the movies. I wanted her to say, "You are cured." She would never say this. Even my students weren't naïve enough to write those kinds of stories. I closed my eyes, "Let's do it."

Nurse Navigator untied the back of my gown and it fell to reveal a tight brace, not unlike a corset, around my chest and abdomen. I noticed that my left arm was numb. I did not know it would remain this way for the rest of my life. (Days later, I would wake in the night and call the hospital, convinced I was having a stroke.) She unhooked the brace and I felt my breasts fall; I looked at the ceiling.

"My dad," I said, trembling, "has a scar that runs from his sternum to his navel, thick as a ribbon."

Working the gauze, Nurse Navigator lifted her eyebrows. "Oh, yeah?"

I nodded. "Kept him out of Vietnam, that surgery. He had gangrene," I told her. "How someone gets gangrene in their stomach is beyond me. Then again, I guess gangrene was better than Vietnam ... "

"Have a look," Nurse Navigator said.

I stared stubbornly at the ceiling. "First, tell me how it looks," I said, "on a scale of one to 'seriously deformed.'"

Nurse Navigator laughed. "She did a wonderful job. Go on, have a look."

I took a deep breath, turned my gaze downward and saw the purple breast, the tight black line of stitches where my nipple had been, a hemline between life and death.

For all that the absence signified, I had been expecting something far more dramatic, something bloody, mangled and gaping. Rather, I had been hoping for as much. I longed to have a big reaction. I wanted an incision that would warrant hair pulling, fist shaking, agonized cries of "What hath God wrought?!" Instead, I slowly pulled my gown back up over my shoulders, mumbled, "Not bad."

It wasn't bad. Nor was it good. No matter how tidy science and medicine are with their sterilization, their careful lasers, their precise scopes, their lexicons of cells and dosages, I was still staring down a gland that looked like it had had its ass kicked in a bar fight.

But it wasn't really like that, or like anything else.

"Are you okay?" asked Nurse Navigator.

"It'll take some getting used to," I told her.

"It will," she said. "But you have to realize that this is you now."

I stared down at my gowned chest. In the night I'd

remembered, fondly, that teardrop of a breast, lifted into countless cotton bras, rubbed in showers, and held in the hands of lovers. In the night, I swore I'd felt a phantom nipple harden in the cold.

Beneath the cloth, bandages squared my left breast. "Yeah," I told Nurse Navigator. "It is me."

"It is," she replied, pleased by my concession.

I glanced down the opening of my shirt. "But it looks nothing like the brochure."

Bernie

When my friend Jon got his Boston Terrier, he became obsessed with the breed, blurting factoids about Boston Terriers to anyone who would listen:

"Did you know Boston Terriers were the first non-sporting dog breed in the US?"

"Gerald Ford had a Boston Terrier, as did Helen Keller."

"In some versions of *The Wizard of Oz,* Toto is a Boston Terrier."

One night, Jon dropped a "lesser known fact about Boston Terriers" into some conversation a group of us was having and my friend Megan eyed him. "Jon," she said, "hate to break it to you, but no one cares about Boston Terriers."

After that, we took to teasing Jon ruthlessly, interrupting him mid-sentence to say things like, "Jon, did you know that Boston Terriers were the first dog to fight in the War on Terror?"

Jon developed a nasty Vicodin habit unrelated to our teasing, went off to rehab in Minnesota, and no one ever heard from him again. When I adopted my Dachshund, Bernie, I thought about Jon for the first time in many years and one afternoon, on the phone with Megan, said, "Did you know Dachshunds are thought to hold the cure for cancer?"

Megan laughed, "Then I guess your dog has one redeeming quality."

When first introduced to Megan, Bernie snapped at her.

"Your dog's a racist," she proclaimed. "He hates me because I'm Irish."

"That's very retro," I replied.

"Stupid German dog," she muttered. "Bernie Hitler."

Whenever I complained about living in Milwaukee, Megan would say, "I bet Bernie Hitler feels right at home with all the German beer halls."

I had to move to Milwaukee. I was offered a job with a paycheck that would allow me to quit three of my other jobs; it came with health insurance, and as much as I didn't want to leave Chicago, I also didn't want to spend another year regarding the emergency room at Cook County Hospital a "primary care facility." In the end, it was all very fortuitous. Two months after my move to Milwaukee, three days after my fancy new health insurance kicked in, I found a small mass in my left breast that turned out to be a Stage II cancer.

My whole adult life I had wanted my own dog, but prior to my Milwaukee job I could hardly afford to feed myself, much less an animal. I had a vision of the exact dog I wanted—a fluffy white Maltese puppy I would name Edith. Edith would be quiet and clean. Edith would be well-behaved and dignified. For some people, it's the car or the house or the kids. For me, being "grown up" meant Edith. When I moved to Milwaukee, I felt safe in the knowledge that by my thirty-fifth birthday, I would have arrived: a full-time teaching position and Edith.

After my diagnosis, I stopped thinking about Edith. All dreams were temporarily deferred. I slogged through my classes. I stopped paying my utility bills. I stopped watching movies. I stopped writing. When some of the abject horror began to dissolve, I found remnants of a life placed on pause: a half-smoked pack of Camel Lights in a drawer, a play I'd begun writing still open in an unsaved Word document, an unsent birthday card to a friend stamped and addressed, my Netflix queue asking, "Resume watching *Delicatessen*?"

The first normal activity I resumed in earnest was reading. I had to read. I felt like a fraud as a thinker, as a writer, if I wasn't reading. But then I'd start a novel and find myself unable to empathize with any of the characters. *What are you whining about?* I'd think. *Oh, yes, your marriage is falling apart. Oh, yes. How very sad. Well, I had cancer.*

So I started reading dog books and rekindling my plan for Edith, because the only plan that felt comforting was my plan for Edith. I'd take her to dog parks, I'd buy her sweaters.

After my diagnosis, I had two surgeries in quick succession. The last was to install a port, a length of tubing that would allow chemotherapy to be pumped efficiently through my bloodstream, and it was while recovering from that surgery that I began reading a book about dog training written by monks, figuring it would satisfy both my need to fantasize about dog ownership and my need for spiritual comfort.

I brought this book into the examination room after my second surgery. When my doctor entered, I tried to shove the book into my backpack. I had told this woman I was a writer, an instructor of English—and as such I should've been reading Chekhov or Munro or some obscure, albeit intellectually ferocious, prose-poem. Of course, she asked what I'd been reading, what I'd been frantically stuffing back into my bag. The way I'd acted, it could have been animal pornography.

"Dog book," I mumbled.

"Cookbook?" she asked.

I shook my head. "Do you think I could get a dog?" I said.

My surgeon squinted, like she didn't understand the question.

"I mean, I don't want to get a dog and like, you know, die on it."

She smiled, touched my knee. "You can get a dog," she said. "You're not going to die on it."

I felt such relief, almost giddy at the assurance that at thirty-four I might outlive a dog.

During treatment, what I feared—second only to agonizing, early death—was loss of my independence. I did not want to be cared for by friends and family. I did not want people in my space. Phone calls, fine. Brief visits, fine. But I didn't want anyone making me chicken soup or tucking me into bed. I was almost unreasonable on this point, convinced that if someone came to help me, I would be doomed to die.

"No," I told my mother the day of my first chemotherapy treatment. "You're not coming here. I'll call you when I'm done." I'd seen *Terms of Endearment*. I knew what happened when cancer patients let their mothers care for them: they died. Thinking it funny, I made this remark to one of the oncology nurses who had observed I was at my treatment alone.

"Yeah," I said. "My mom wanted to come, but I've seen *Terms of Endearment*."

The nurse smiled weakly and looked down at my paperwork. I was used to this. From the moment I was diagnosed, it was as though I was in an episode of *The Twilight Zone* where, no matter how hard I tried, no one was able to register my sense of humor.

The day of my biopsy, as I lay on the table, positioned and probed by the radiologist, I heard the lab technician enter, then the sound of glass clinking as he prepared the slides for my cells, and I joked, "Any chance someone's making me a martini?"

To which the radiologist matter-of-factly replied, "That's the lab tech."

The day the nurse handed me a thick pink tome entitled *Your Breast Cancer Handbook,* I laughed at the title— "Does this, like, show me how to use breast cancer to get out of a lease early, or avoid going to a baby shower?"

The laughter was nervous, polite.

A co-worker, a cancer survivor, asked how much chemotherapy I would have to receive, and instead of saying, "a lot," I made reference to an episode of *The Cosby Show,* replied, "It's gonna be 'chug-a-lug, Vanessa' for me."

My co-worker looked at me like I was mad, blurted, "You don't drink chemo!"

I blinked dumbly. I knew this. Even before I had cancer, I knew chemotherapy was not ingested by way of a straw like a Capri Sun juice box.

But cancer at thirty-four was also the most unexpected, unfunny thing in the world. I was a hypochondriac. I believed hypochondriacs didn't really get cancer, they only *thought* they had it. As a hypochondriac, I had imagined, countless times, how I would react if I was ever faced with "bad medical news." I used to joke with Megan, "If it's ever the 'Big C,' I'll get some rusty gun and go out to the shed . . . "

I tried to stop making so many jokes because I didn't want to be mistaken for "sassy-cancer-patient." But I wasn't sure how I should embrace my new status. How I should wear it, clothe myself, my life. Motifs drew the chaos of my writing together, so I sought the same from cancer. I observed my cohort. Some people layered cancer over the parts of themselves that had come before: lawyer, jogger, mom. They purchased trinkets from Susan G. Komen—bracelets and pins and t-shirts that announced their predicament. Others dashed for The Man Upstairs, became fanatically religious, believed in surgery, radiation, and the healing power of prayer. Others joined support groups where women sat around in folding chairs, ate store-bought cookies, squeezed hands, and cried about the mess cancer had made of their lives.

"Respite," a nurse told me. "You need to find your respite."

The week my hair started falling out, I received an email from my friend Kay: a coworker and her husband had taken in an orphaned mini Dachshund named Bernie after his owner had died.

"I know it's not fluffy Edith," Kay wrote, "but he's only five months-old, and a cutie."

In the attached picture, Bernie sat looking up nervously. He had a crooked left ear and wrinkles above his sad, brown eyes. He looked sort of pathetic. I could relate: in three short months, I'd gone from healthy thirty-something who smoked and drank and lifted weights four days a week to a woman who—to say nothing of her nipple and much of her left breast—had lost fifteen pounds, who chewed forestfuls of toothpicks to supplant her longing for cigarettes, who put extra bags of chamomile in her hot water to compensate for her need to "overdo it." Who was, some days, run so ragged from those noxious chemicals she could barely manage the task of making herself a grilled cheese sandwich.

The first time I spoke to Bernie's foster parent, Shawn, on the phone, he talked at length about how sad his wife was to part with Bernie. She wanted to keep him, he said, and then scoffed, "Chicks." *Oh, Bernie*, I thought. *Your foster home must be rife with sexism.*

There were some political passions that had abandoned me post-cancer, but feminism was not one of them. My feminism only intensified in the world of breast cancer treatment—a disease dressed in pink, infantilized and trivialized by campaigns like "Save the Ta-Ta's," the cancer regarded in popular culture as a mere ugly blossom on the gaudy tree of heterosexual womanhood; as a youngish, single, gender-ambivalent lesbian, I became quickly and acutely attuned to the ways of *Breastcancerland*, and I did not care for its customs.

Shawn's dismissive remark about his wife's genuine sadness at parting with the dog made me bristle, but I hid my feelings because I wanted Bernie.

The day I was to meet and adopt the dog, Shawn called.

"Caved into the old lady," he said. "I'm whipped."

Pre-cancer, such news would have deflated me for days. Post-cancer, it was a bit like hearing, "We're all out of ranch dressing." In the universe of bad news, cancer is the Oscar. After you've gotten the Oscar, it's hard to feel depressed about not getting a Golden Globe.

A month later, however, I received an email from a woman named Corrie. Subject line: "Bernie." Corrie was Shawn's wife and she explained that they had decided, for certain, to part with Bernie; was I still interested?

I was deeply skeptical, convinced there was something horribly wrong with the dog. He must have some fatal flaw, and considering my own literal fatal flaw, I wasn't about to take in an animal with a figurative one. I phoned Corrie and asked her why they wanted to be rid of Bernie.

"Shawn says," she began, "that we've got enough going on with the kids. Shawn says we don't have time for Bernie."

If I couldn't help Corrie, at least I could rescue her dog.

I met Shawn at his trucking company on the southwest side of Milwaukee. I had to take two buses to get there. And it was my birthday. As usual, when alone in public, I wore my newsboy cap to safeguard myself against the are-you-bald-by-choice-or-cancer-bald stares. With my news-boy cap, I wasn't a cancer patient, I was merely a dyke on a bus.

When I arrived at the trucking company, it was just me and Shawn.

"Corrie's lost," he scowled. "She's only been here ten freaking times before." He shook his head, then added, with disgust, "Girls."

I bit my tongue. To keep from having to hear him make more disparaging remarks about his wife, I asked Shawn for Bernie's backstory. He told me their neighbor had purchased Bernie from a breeder, "When he thought he had beat cancer."

I felt myself tense up. Shawn and his wife knew nothing of my medical circumstances. All they knew was that I was a woman in the market for a dog.

"Then he died," Shawn said. "Guess he didn't beat the cancer."

"Guess not," I said, tugging on my cap to make sure it wasn't sliding. A superstition gripped me: Bernie's original owner died of cancer. If I take Bernie, I will die of cancer, too. Curse of the cancer dog. I wanted to call the whole thing off. But as I worked to formulate a believable excuse as to why I had to leave right then and there, Corrie arrived with Bernie in her arms.

The first time I had chemo, the oncology nurse, in an attempt to distract me, calm me, pointed to my iPod and asked, "What's your favorite music?" And I told her, "I don't have favorites. I just have things I don't like."

And this is true. And Bernie wasn't Edith, but he also was not something I disliked.

I wasn't yet on the second bus home when I called Corrie and told her I only needed two days before I could bring Bernie into my house. "I have some work stuff going on," I lied.

Really, I had chemo. I didn't want her to know. I didn't want Shawn to know and for my cancer treatment to become a reason for them to reconsider. So I spent my birthday shopping for dog items—rawhide bones, squeaky toys, expensive organic kibble—and I spent the day after my birthday hooked up to an IV drip at the cancer center, dreaming of Bernie-who-was-not-Edith.

The day after chemo, I took a cab to Shawn's trucking company and picked up Bernie in his little crate. Shawn handed me a paper bag. "Corrie made this," he said, explaining that the bag contained Bernie's favorite blanket and a tennis ball and "some stupid dog card she had to run out and buy special."

"That's *nice*," I said emphatically. I wanted him to know that the gesture of the card was *nice*. I wanted him to regard his wife, in this, as thoughtful, not stupid.

That first day with Bernie, I was full of pain; both emotional and physical. I felt sorry for Corrie. Her card made it clear she had not wanted to part with the dog, and I felt like I was colluding with Shawn. Then I thought of Bernie's first owner, dead of cancer. I knew not what kind of cancer. I knew nothing else about this man but that he was dead from cancer and had purchased Bernie after he thought he had conquered the disease. I had to force myself to stop thinking about it, because the thought broke my heart.

Then, of course, I was in chemo-pain. The irony of chemotherapy is that the drug that could cure you is also the drug that could very well kill you. Until chemotherapy entered my life, I felt perfectly healthy. I hadn't had so much as a head cold in over a year. My body was in seemingly marvelous shape despite my years of smoking. On the list of pernicious chemo side effects is heart failure and leukemia, and I remember reading these in my oncologist's office the day of my first treatment, weeping as I signed a waiver that basically said, "I understand chemotherapy may kill me, but I want it anyway."

The day of Bernie's arrival, I felt that chemo might kill me. The second phase of my treatment involved a drug that, in addition to exhaustion, brought about nerve pain—like electrically charged rubber-bands snapping at random intervals throughout my body—sometimes in the skull, sometimes the spine, sometimes the shins, sometimes, inexplicably, the ankles.

"My ankles are killing," I told Megan one day, early on in the second phase of chemo.

"Well," Megan said, "maybe you never had breast cancer. Maybe you had ankle cancer."

We loved the idea of "ankle cancer."

Dumbest and best cancer ever, we concluded.

What are you doing? I thought that first night. *This isn't Edith. You're killing yourself over some second-hand wiener-dog. No one gets a second-hand dog in the middle of chemotherapy. This is the dumbest thing you've ever done.*

That night, Bernie and I went to bed at eight-thirty. I did not feel well. I put his crate at the foot of my bed and he readily climbed inside.

I fell quickly into a deep sleep and dreamt of walking through my old neighborhood in Chicago. Pleasant at first, and then, in the dream, I stepped over a pile of dog shit. Then another. And another. And as I walked, in my dream, the smell of dog shit was oppressive, inescapable, unbearable. There was dog shit everywhere. Suddenly my nostalgic dream had morphed into a fecal nightmare.

As I startled awake into the dark of my Milwaukee bedroom that also reeked of dog shit, I worried for a moment that I was trapped in some strange, chemo-brain reality where I could see my waking life, but still smell my nightmare. Then I heard Bernie whimpering in his crate. I leapt up from my bed so fast, a spike of pain shot from the base of my spine to the top of my head and I cried out, fumbled for the latch on Bernie's crate—a crate he had shat in, most explosively.

He crawled out slowly, and I scooped him up into my arms, ran into the kitchen and frantically clipped him to his leash. Together we hobbled out into the alley.

Watching Bernie relieve himself, I waved the plastic bag helplessly in my hand. This was not the sort of mess I could pick up. *Great,* I thought. *My new dog is dying. I am a cancer patient and my new dog is dying. Was I Mussolini in a past life?*

Carrying Bernie back into the apartment, I was overwhelmed by the smell. Chemo sometimes makes even pleasant scents nauseating, and now, confronted with the cruel stench of dog shit, I was starting to retch. I set Bernie down on my bed and raced to the bathroom, but the feces-contaminated crate sat stinking in the corner. I had to get it out or get it clean. I had no yard, no hose; there was only the bathtub. From beneath the sink I grabbed a bottle of Dawn dishwashing liquid and poured it in. I climbed into the tub with Bernie's sloshing crate that now looked like an oil spill diorama.

Then from my bedroom came four distinct gulping sounds. I eased my aching body up and into the hall. From there I could see four tidy piles of vomit hillocked across my clean sheets.

"I give up," I told Bernie, crumpling to the floor. I tugged the sheet off my bed and Bernie came sliding with it into my lap. I hauled us up onto the bare mattress.

"We're going to bed now," I announced. "No more shitting. No more puking."

I placed a pillow over each of our faces and the false dark eventually put us to sleep, the cancer patient and the queasy Dachshund.

In the morning, I limped to the kitchen and made Bernie a breakfast of brown rice and scrambled eggs. I had read somewhere the combination eased a dog's upset stomach.

"I read somewhere," Megan once teased Jon, "that it was Boston Terriers, not Churchill, who ended World War II..." By then, Jon had grown defensive over our jokes about his dog. He gave Megan the finger, told her to fuck off.

At first, Bernie refused to eat so I got down on my knees, scooped the crumbly mess into my hands and offered it to him. "Look here, dog, no one is dying up in this apartment—and that includes you." Eventually, Bernie strained forward and took small bites from my hands.

"You barfed on my sheets," I reminded him as he ate. "I've been a cancer patient for six months, I've taken some potent drugs, and even I haven't barfed on my sheets."

I regarded him as we sat there on the kitchen floor. He was red and oddly shaped. Not even remotely Edith. "You're not exactly what I had in mind," I told him.

Then again, nothing that had happened that year was what I'd had in mind. No one ever has a plan that includes cancer: *Oh, I don't know. Think I'll move to Milwaukee for a year or so, save some money, check out the local color, get a little cancer...*

But then I guess that was the joke, that was Bernie. Here was the objective correlative for all that had happened since I'd moved to Milwaukee. Here was my red dog, my black joke, my respite. I laughed, and sifted scramble between my fingers.

"This," I said to Bernie, "is some fucked up shit."

Jesus Never Made Me a Mix-Tape

"When I die," Josephine said, "I want to be laid out in the woods and pecked apart by birds."

I laughed, but Josephine—my best friend and partner in hilarity—shook her head and grew serious.

"Like a Buddhist," she said.

I nodded, solemnly.

"What about outer space?" she said.

"What about it?"

"It wouldn't be so bad to die in space."

I considered the question for a moment. When I was ten, I'd expressed a simple wish to Jesus in gym class. That morning our science teacher had shown us an episode of *Cosmos,* where Carl Sagan, in his trademark turtleneck, assured me that even Earth, like humans, had an expiration date. As for me, I was ten already. A decade old. I found this unsettling. I looked at the small crucifix on the west wall of the gym, clasped my hands in my lap, and made a request: *A rhino, a rabid dog, spontaneous combustion, even crucified like you—whatever it is, just not in a bed. Don't let me die in a bed.* It was bad enough, I thought, that one had to die in a body.

To die in space would be pretty spectacular—weightless among the stars, diminishing. Your bones could float forever with the satellites—part of the galaxy instead of the earth.

"Space," I told Josephine. "Or birds. Either would be better than dying in a hospital bed, where the last words you're going to hear will be 'increase the morphine.'"

When she called me morbid, I reminded Josephine that she was the one who had expressed a desire to be pecked asunder by birds. For years after this, I believed it was standard Buddhist procedure to lay the corpse on a forest floor, cover it in birdseed and wait for the crows, sparrows, and cardinals to do their job. I was familiar only with the Catholic approach and forced to choose between the jaws of a casket and a beak, I, too, preferred the idea of birds.

Of course, this isn't really standard Buddhist burial custom.

In my early twenties, under the tutelage of a former professor, I experimented with Buddhism. At the time, I was suffering from panic attacks and a deep aversion to the psychiatric methods that might alleviate them. Having told my professor of my affliction, she made me my first set of mala beads and explained how to use them, what to say, how to breathe.

"What's this? Don't know," she said, pinching each bead between thumb and forefinger, sliding along the band, like saying the Rosary.

Years later, in my early thirties, I resurrected the mala beads and the mantra. I clutched them through MRIs, rolled them in my lap during consultations with surgeons and oncologists. At night, lying in bed, I chanted, "What's this? Don't know. What's this? Don't know," until my speculations, projections and predictions burnt off like a fog.

Rocks do not reproduce, read the opening line of the textbook for fifth grade sex ed. *Nor do computers.* The list went on, offering forth an exhaustive catalogue of the many things on Planet Earth that are incapable of reproduction. Sex ed separated the boys from the girls. The boys took their lessons with the principal and Father O'Brien. The girls remained with Sister Enid and the female history teacher. By then, Sister Enid was well into her seventies, and the history teacher was a hard sixty, white-haired and dour. An empty Hills Brothers can was passed around the room, into which we anonymously slipped our most pressing questions about our bodies, reproduction, and sex itself. I treated the can like a Magic Eight Ball, asking, "When will I get my period?"

Skyscrapers cannot reproduce, nor can lakes . . .

I was unsure where the list was leading. I had, in recent months, managed to piece together that sex and babies were somehow linked. My friends and I discussed the correlation in short, secretive bursts. We shared tidbits of information that inched in around the facts. It wasn't that different from the textbook. *Houses do not reproduce, cars do not reproduce.* A process of elimination. *Stones do not reproduce, television, and model horses do not reproduce.* A means of erasing the world until only the small obscenity of our own bodies was left.

The home I grew up in was devoutly Catholic. We attended mass every Sunday. We ate fish on Fridays during Lent. My first Communion photo hung in the living room, a crucifix hung above my bed. As a child, I viewed Jesus as a nice imaginary friend with whom I could confer privately whether in crisis or bored in class.

In my mind, Jesus tended to side with me—assuring me I was fine to go on doodling horse-heads in the margin of my math notebook while my teacher spoke, telling me I'd never need long division, telling me horse portraiture was the more critical skill to master. He was the permissive, doting parent who assured me I could do anything I liked, because I was quiet, a believer, a "good girl."

For a nickel at a parish rectory sale, I scored a Sacred Heart of Jesus statue. The figure was plastic, the size of a Barbie Doll, and I kept him on my nightstand—his red and white robes opened to reveal a protruding, crowned heart. This was the last image I saw before I slept, the first I saw when I woke, his face a benevolent inquiry, "Did you get your full eight hours?"

"If they didn't kill Jesus," I once asked Sister Enid, "would he have lived forever?"

It was Ash Wednesday; our class had just returned from mass where the priest had thumbed stubby crosses onto our foreheads. This was my least favorite holy day because it was messy and revolved around the fact of mortality. If I came from ashes and dust, I certainly could not remember and had no desire to return to them.

Sister Enid used my question to remind the whole class that Jesus was human. "Skin and bones," she said. "Just like you and me."

I was disappointed. "So he would have died eventually?"

"Just like you and me," she repeated.

From the pew, I'd stare at the statue behind the altar. In my mind's eye, Jesus was a soft-spoken, relatively easy-going fellow, like my dad. Above the altar, he was a dead man—pale and so thin I could count his ribs; his head flopped to one side in divine exhaustion, bleeding from his hands, feet and head.

"The body is just a body," the teachers told us. "The body is a temporary vessel; the soul is what matters. The soul lives forever." We were reminded of this, especially, when catastrophe struck—a priest developed lung cancer, a beloved teacher died in her sleep, several parishioners were poisoned by cyanide-tainted Tylenol. The Challenger exploded.

We dismissed the body, glorified its destruction—honored histories of flagellation, of martyrs burned and mutilated. We cannibalized Christ every Sunday, and fixated on the grisliest aspects of His murder: the spear in the side, the lashings, the crown of thorns dug into the skull, as though, at best, the body was built for torment.

There were moments during the first few months after my diagnosis when I thought about revisiting Jesus, when I thought about calling on him for a little assistance. But then, given our extended separation, reaching out felt rude—Christ was not, after all, a divine panic button. By that stage, Jesus was just another famous dead guy with a beard. I'd have about as much luck necromancing Abraham Lincoln or late-stage Jim Morrison. But I wanted to believe that cancer was part of some larger plan, that a divine entity would see me through, would not let me down, would not let me die.

On Josephine's bedroom wall hung a giant poster of Perry Farrell in the crucifix pose. We sat beneath the blasphemous image, smoking Marlboro Lights, Jane's Addiction blaring. Josephine nudged my rib. "Do you want me to show you how I kiss guys?"

"Oh," I replied. "I know how to kiss guys. I've done it before."

Josephine threw her head back and laughed maniacally.

But I was telling the truth. I did know. At sixteen, I had kissed exactly one boy, a mutual friend of ours. He drove me home one night in his father's station wagon and asked if he could kiss me. Figuring this an eventuality, something I might as well get out of the way, I consented. His face was rough. He smelled of sandalwood and marijuana, and while he kissed me, I stared at the digital dashboard clock, resigning myself to a life of utter boredom with men.

"I'm not asking you if you ever kissed a guy," Josephine clarified. "I'm asking you if you want to see how I do it."

I was confused. Why did I need to know how she kissed boys? Was this a favor? Was there a correct method? Something else to be approached as a science? I pulled a fresh Marlboro from our shared pack and lit it. I'd already learned to smoke away my nerves. "Why?" I asked.

"Because I want to kiss you," Josephine said.

Though I found Josephine vastly more interesting than any boy I knew, not to mention much more aesthetically pleasing, the thought of kissing her had never occurred to me until that moment. I felt sudden desire coupled with a strong need to suppress it. "It's probably not a good idea," I said, apologetically.

She kissed me anyway, and I kissed back.

Cancer is a form of "cell immortality." On the surface, this sounds great; if we're made of cells and if our cells are immortal then it stands to reason that we'll live forever. The problem, of course, is that cells are meant to die. No cell is supposed to stick around too long. We shed them constantly—hair falls out, skin chafes—and, biologically speaking, this is good. Chemotherapy forces, or attempts to force, every rapidly dividing cell to die. This accounts for the hair loss and—in many younger women—menopause.

I was warned that in the course of a necessary war, "Red Devil" chemo would make collateral damage of my perfectly healthy ovaries. Dr. S, my oncologist, a woman roughly my age, asked me about "harvesting my eggs." *Harvesting*—the word made me feel like a baby crop about to go to seed.

"No thanks," I said.

I had always expected that my biological clock would one day loudly alarm, expected that one morning I'd awaken to find I craved babies as I craved food and sex, as vampires crave blood, as zombies crave brains. Similarly, I always expected I'd someday be interested in men.

I wondered about my own genetic inheritance. I pictured a paddock scene in twelfth century Eastern Europe, where a peasant woman with gigantic breasts and a dozen crying babies fathered by a lazy husband with bad teeth, threw down her pitchfork and proclaimed, "Fuck this shit forever."

"Don't make any rash decisions," Dr. S advised, as though, at thirty-four, I'd never before seriously considered the question of children.

"I'm not," I assured her. "I just want to go forward with treatment."

What I meant was that I wanted those cells to die.

The Sunday after I kissed Josephine, I went to mass with my parents. There was none of the customary teen-aged complaining—I was up and at the ready, waiting on the porch before my father had started the car. Surprised by my eagerness, my mother teased, "What's the occasion? Did you kill someone?"

After Communion, on my knees, I prayed to my old pal, Jesus. *It was a mistake,* I explained. *She tricked me. What can I do? Give me a sign.*

I imagined Jesus' response, *Dear, sweet child, you're not gay. But your friend Josephine? Totally gay.*

Kneeling in the pew, hands tightly clasped, all I could hear was blood rushing in my ears. *I'm sorry,* I silently lamented. *This is the worst thing I've ever done.* But the silence—that rushing in my ears—was condemnation enough. Jesus wasn't talking.

Outside the church, I felt angry. What was so great about Jesus? He'd never made me a mix-tape, never sat up half the night smoking cigarettes on the swing set in the park. Jesus never wrote my name in the frost on car windows, never smuggled rum into my bedroom, smelling like Marlboros and Chanel No. 5, and He never laughed at my jokes.

Love became its own kind of religion, an incurable fanaticism full of ritual and idolatry, its own fragile faith. Still, some nights I'd lie awake worrying, *Oh God, what am I going to do about Jesus?* For a year, I juggled two distinctly different relationships, torn between what Jesus wanted and what I wanted. But by the time I had completely stopped talking to Jesus, Josephine had met a boy she liked better than me.

"It's not like we could really be together," she told me. "It's not like we could get married or something."

"This isn't even a real thing," I concurred.

And in 1992 that felt true.

The week I was diagnosed, I dragged the mattress off my bed frame and into the living room. If I was going to die, I did not want to die in a bed. I slept fitfully on my living room floor, the television always on. I woke at odd hours to weather reports, infomercials for food processors, and re-runs of *Good Times*.

One night, I awoke to a televangelist who spoke about a septuagenarian dying of stomach cancer.

"Folks," the pastor said, "do you know what that man says? He says, 'There but for the grace of God go I.'"

Where, I wondered, was the "grace of God" in getting cancer at thirty-four? Where was the "grace" in surgeries that butchered the most tender parts of my body, in the bi-weekly chemo appointments that made my skin turn gray, that made me go bald, that buckled my knees and made even sushi and milkshakes taste like metallic dog shit? The Jesus-minded, of course, would say the "grace of God" was in my survival, but survival is anything but graceful. I thought of my grandmother, who died in a bed.

The year before she was diagnosed with Alzheimer's, when she was eighty-two and I was twenty-seven, she stood over her kitchen sink, rinsing a coffee pot, and asked me whether or not I believed there was an afterlife. I shrugged, the question made me uncomfortable; I loved her, and I didn't want to think about her dying.

"Just tell me," she said. "What do you think happens when we die?"

"Scientists say we're energy," I said, "and because of that, we can't really be destroyed."

She smiled. The sun was coming in through the window above the sink. Just beyond where she stood birds landed on the feeder, paused briefly to steal seeds then flew off.

On my floor, in the blue glow of the television, I remembered Carl Sagan's "star stuff" and thought that if we went before the grace of anything, it was not God, but science.

It was hard for me to imagine my body living long after the cancer. Friends wondered aloud if that was why I had chosen not to store some eggs. "You just don't know," one said. "Someday, you might want that piece of immortality."

But I didn't see it this way—I wasn't opting out of immortality, I was opting out of a pricey, limited warranty on my DNA. Why create someone with my proclivity for sunburns, fiscal irresponsibility, and cancer? Why bring forth progeny with my affinity for cigarettes, prescription pills, and French Fries? I was busy enough contending with the atoms, molecules and particles that billions of years of evolution had allocated me. Most days, my own "star stuff" was almost more than I could bear. A good reason, I thought, to remain committed to my body, alone, on earth, for however many years I had left.

I took up singing in the shower; my imitation of country-western songs: tuneless ditties about the things that were leaving me.

Nipple done left ain't never comin' back . . .
It's the tenth o' the month, don't get my period no more . . .
Well, it's Friday in the cit-tay and I've only got one eyebrow . . .
One of the grade school nuns told us kids that our singing pleased God, that it was better than simply reciting prayers. "The Lord loves song," she told us. Of course, this

didn't apply to all song. In junior high we were roundly chastised for listening to Madonna and the boys who smuggled a 2LiveCrew tape into the school were threatened with expulsion.

When I was a teenager, one of my aunts told me that the year after I was born, NASA sent Voyager into space along with a golden record on which was a small music sampling from Earth. One of the songs on the album was Blind Willie Johnson's "Dark Was the Night, Cold Was the Ground."

"I don't know that song," I told my aunt.

"It's a sad song," she said. "It was meant to demonstrate human loneliness."

Why? I thought, but didn't ask. *Why would you want to demonstrate loneliness to aliens? Why not joy or peace or love?*

I was thirty before I actually heard "Dark Was the Night, Cold Was the Ground." The slide guitar was twangy and slow. Blind Willie's voice was gravelly. There were no lyrics, as he did nothing but moan and hum. Though I tried to forget it, the song haunted me for years. When I closed my eyes, I'd see that slide guitar, that sound like celestial tracers flaring through the sky. Immortalized though his song may be, Blind Willie died of malarial fever in his burnt out house, in a bed, on a wet mattress.

Two dances with the Red Devil, twice that cellular napalm coursed through my veins, torching every atom in its path, and my period stopped. Maxi-pads collected dust under the bathroom sink. I woke in the night, kicking off blankets, face throbbing, sweat tingling my cheeks.

"Menopause," Dr. S told me. "Hot flashes. Perfectly normal."

This was the end of me. *Stereos can't reproduce, books can't reproduce. Allison can't reproduce, either.* Nothing but my philodendron would live on after me—and even that wouldn't live long without proper care.

If I was ever asked again about that "little piece of immortality," if anyone ever asked why I didn't want that, I knew my reply.

"I wanted to live."

Speaking to Strangers

I could not tell you the color of my first lover's eyes, or of my mother's eyes, or even the eyes of my brother or nieces, but I can say this with certainty: Maeve's eyes were brown. I attribute my memory of this detail to my vantage point. I was always flat on my back.

Maeve's eyes were a destination—warm, wet sand, tree roots—a bright coast I could glimpse but never really reach.

There were moments, in those early months after my diagnosis, when nothing felt still, when everything rippled like water—bobbing, restless—nowhere to plant myself firmly. Those days, the best I could do was hope the waves stayed small.

I once read an article about Virginia Woolf attending a dinner party with a priest. The priest was at a far end of the table, discussing his travels, and Woolf could only pick up snippets of what he said.

At one point during the dinner party, the priest said he could "see the whole coast."

Woolf, skeptical of religious men, mishearing him, asked, "And where is the Holy Ghost?"

The priest, in turn, looked at her incredulously and replied, "Why, wherever the sea is."

* * *

After a reading for an anthology in which I'd published a story, a woman approached me. I'd noticed the woman earlier, when she'd entered the bookstore, because she was cute and kind of my type. When she walked up to me, I figured she'd tell me she liked my story, figured I'd turn a little red, reply, "Thank you, that means a lot to me."

But she didn't tell me she liked my story; she told me she "loved" it, cracked the anthology open a little too easily to page seventy-four, handed me a pen and asked me to sign.

Self-consciously, I scribbled my name next to the title of my piece, and handed the book back to my "fan."

The editor of the anthology introduced each writer before she or he read, and when she introduced me, she mentioned that I had, only a year earlier, moved to Milwaukee from Chicago. Remembering this detail, The Fan asked me how I liked Milwaukee.

I replied quickly, "I hate it."

"Hate it?" The Fan balked. "Hate it? How can you hate Milwaukee?" Without prompting, The Fan rattled off all the things she loved about Milwaukee. The list was long, remarkably unimpressive, and included "winter."

Maybe, my best friend Emily once gently suggested, *people don't like it when you openly insult the place where they want to live.*

I tried to be cognizant of this while The Fan was excitedly cataloguing her affinity for Milwaukee—Pizzaman, Brady Street, Old German Beer Hall.

When she was through, I watched her a moment, felt myself weighing the decision—to love winter, or not to love winter.

*　*　*

Maeve laughed when I complained about Milwaukee. I would arrive to a morning appointment, freezing or rain-soaked or both, narrow my eyes and declare, "Milwaukee is a treasure and a delight." Or, "I love the sting of the lake wind—like being slapped by a thousand tiny hands."

When I found out I had cancer, friends, family, and co-workers seemed uncomfortable, almost baffled by my jokes. Most wanted me to be grave and grateful, wanted me to stop saying things like, "Chemo is an excellent weight loss supplement."

When they did laugh, I'd hear the strain of obligation, and I was loath to be humored.

Of course, I did wonder to what extent Maeve's laughter was also obligatory, part of her job; I was her patient and so, for all intents and purposes, her customer—and a regular at that. We didn't meet; I was assigned.

"You really love winter?" I asked The Fan.

"Oh, I do," she affirmed, wide-eyed, hungry for the start of that brutal season.

I shook my head and laughed. "Wow."

Boldly, she touched one of my forearms. "You don't have to love winter," she said, "but I'm going to help you love Milwaukee."

"Help me love," suggested I was *trying* to love Milwaukee. On the contrary, I was not trying. I did not want to love Milwaukee, because I had already decided to hate it.

Nevertheless, I said nothing, smiled politely. She was flirting. I understood this. I admired this. I'd never been good at flirting. Flirting was hard for me, mostly because it usually manifested as a kind of indentured servitude—help with laundry, feedback on a poem, hauling boxes of records up five-story walkups in July.

The weekend before I moved to Milwaukee, Emily took me out dancing. Emily was straight, but she took me to a gay dance club, hoping to find me a "farewell fuck" from Chicago.

I wasn't in the mood to dance that night, and stood in the shadowy borderlands of the dance floor, sipping my vodka tonic, watching bodies shift in the dim blue light.

As I stood there, a woman with wild, curly hair danced toward me in a slight, yellow sundress. "Are you here alone?" she said.

"No," I shouted into her ear. "I'm with a friend."

"Don't you like to dance?" She moved toward me as she spoke, her arms curling upward like smoke ribbons. If she was trying to entice me onto the dance floor, she was failing. Dancing while you spoke was akin, in my book, to being sung to. What was the other person supposed to do? Maintain eye contact and try not to die of awkwardness?

I took a step back. "No, not really."

On the El ride home, Emily punched me in the arm. "You're such a fool," she said. "That woman was totally coming on to you."

But I knew that. "Anyway," I said, "what's the point of getting involved with someone if I'm moving to another city next week?"

"Hooking up is not 'getting involved,'" Emily reminded me.

I slid my foot over a half-eaten can of peaches. "I can hook up in Milwaukee."

I presumed the pickin's might be slimmer in Milwaukee. Maybe the women wouldn't be as appealing as in Chicago.

Lots of mullets and baseball caps among the lesbians in Milwaukee, I predicted; not enough tattoo sleeves, not enough yellow sundresses. But that wasn't really what concerned me. I was mostly worried about the lack of Emilys.

I never actually got the chance to prove or disprove my theory about Milwaukee lesbians. The week before I started treatment, I handed my arm to a nurse who tied a tourniquet and patted up my veins to determine whether or not the surgeon should install a chemo port. My cancer diagnosis was only three weeks old, and every day was full of new astonishment, new horrors that enveloped me unexpectedly, inflating my tongue with confessions I hadn't the wherewithal to suppress.

"I'm never going to have sex again," I blurted.

The nurse paused with her finger pressed to my veins. She looked into my eyes. "You'll be all right."

I was unsure if she was referring to my veins or my sex life, and ashamed now, I wasn't about to ask for clarification.

Sex, of course, was not my primary concern, but sometimes memories of hook-up opportunities, missed and seized, thudded through my mind. I'd run a hand along my numb arm, over my stitched-taut breast and recall how I'd regarded sex as a sort of fast food—available in every city; I can go anywhere, at any time, and get some if I have a taste.

The week before chemo started, unsure if I'd get through alive, I put an ad in the Casual Encounters section of Craigslist: *SWF. 34. Seeking NSA encounter this Saturday.*

My ad was as desperate as it was preposterous. Cancer or not, I wasn't the kind of woman who hocked herself alongside dick pics, pit bull puppies, and couches that smelled of cigarette butts and meth. Dates with people I knew made me nervous, and complete strangers plainly terrified me. And in the end, it didn't matter; when the replies came in, all three, they came two days after chemo had commenced.

Maeve was blonde, a modest dresser—lots of khaki pants and pastel tops, mere hints of makeup. She was plain but not unattractive. She looked like the kind of woman who might identify herself by saying, "I'm a mom ... "

Emily and I had laughed about the commercials for juice and detergent that began with some Maeve-looking woman folding t-shirts or setting out tumblers of Kool-Aid, soberly articulating some inane value and prefacing it with, "I'm a mom, so that means ... "

Emily and I would get going with this, "I'm a mom, so that means I'm against genocide." "I'm a mom, so that means I don't like the idea of nuclear holocaust." "I'm a mom, so that means I like drinking and fucking."

Each maternal non sequitur felt like a condemnation of the people we were not—those with office jobs and mortgages, those who went to church, watched their mouths, bit their tongues.

Shortly after my diagnosis, I joked with Emily, "I'm a mom, so that means I hate having cancer."

Only I laughed.

My first session with Maeve was interrupted by the Nurse Navigator. She wanted to know if I had decided to participate in the clinical trial that involved a full year of chemo. I had chosen not to participate and the admission made me cry.

Maeve stroked my hair, "It's fine. It's okay."

"It *is* okay," Nurse Navigator insisted. "Ninety-six percent of my patients decline participation in clinical trials."

"You don't have a ninety-six percent mortality rate, do you?"

Maeve leaned back into a big throaty laugh. She laughed so hard and for so long that Nurse Navigator shot her a look of disapproval.

"No," said Nurse Navigator. "We do not have a ninety-six percent mortality rate."

Once Nurse Navigator had left, I turned to Maeve. "You liked that one, did you?" I said.

She eyed me with a wide grin. "You slay me."

I spoke to strangers. In the weeks following my diagnosis, I called women I'd never met to talk about their experience with breast cancer, "What stage?" "What treatment?" "How long since...?" Though some conversations continued past midnight, most of their names I no longer remember. I disrobed for doctors and nurses and technicians I would never see again. I attended group appointments where we shared cheap cookies, weak coffee, and intimate details about our medical histories. And once a week, I went to the cancer center and let some woman spend an hour massaging my armpit.

I once asked Maeve how she could stand it: spending that much time in the armpits of strangers.

"Part of my job," she said. "You get used to it."

"Must be a calling," I said. "I can barely stand to speak to strangers, much less touch them."

She bent my arm above my head. "I don't think of my patients as strangers. Do you think of your students as strangers?"

"I guess not," I said. "But then again, I don't have to become intimately acquainted with their body parts. In fact, in my line of work, that's frowned upon."

She laughed. "To each his own."

While I expected cancer to make all my pretentions vanish, to make me humble and tolerant, such was not the case. As though it really mattered anymore, I still winced when someone said, "for all *intensive* purposes," "one in the same," "could care less." I still cringed when confronted with a cliché. I still wanted to scream, "Think about what you're saying!"

But with Maeve, it always seemed she *had* thought about what she was saying and the expression, however dull and familiar, made new and perfect sense.

The Fan's eyes were green.

"So," she said, as the bookstore began to clear, "what are you doing now?"

I was planning to walk home. To do what I now did at night: walk my dog, take my estrogen blocker, and crawl into bed with a book about the plague or the Manson murders or chimpanzees who spoke American Sign Language (cancer made it difficult for me to read anything that wasn't grisly or meaningless).

"Nothing," I said. "You?"

"Want to go somewhere and get a drink or coffee?"

A drink sounded marvelous. Several vodka tonics sounded even better, but I knew that if I drank, I would grow forthcoming. If I grew forthcoming, I'd end up telling The Fan about the cancer, and I didn't want her to know about it. "Coffee," I said.

In her car, a brand new, blue Audi with heated

leather seats and a built-in GPS, she grilled me about my Milwaukee experience, expressing shock at everything I had not done: Summerfest, Film Fest, a Brewer's game, most bars.

"What have you done since you've lived here?"

I looked out the window, laughed a little. "Not much, apparently."

"Worked?" she suggested.

"Yeah," I said, grimly. "Worked."

Two months into my treatment, Emily ditched me.

She did so abruptly, over-the-phone. I was talking about chemo, about the rubber and metal implant just beneath my collarbone.

"It feels weird," I was saying. "I can feel it in my sleep, like there's a dollar's worth of quarters in my chest."

"This is way too intense," Emily interjected in a half-whisper. "This is just way too intense, and that's me; that's my hang-up, I know that."

"What do you mean?" I asked.

"I wish you all the best," she said. "I know you know that."

We didn't really say "goodbye," but her words inferred that this conversation would be our last.

I thought that kind of thing only happened in sentimental movies. I didn't believe friends actually fled when a person got sick. I thought this was a device, a baseless motif. But in the year I was sick, I would lose two close friends for whom the experience proved "too intense." Emily just happened to be the first, so I told Maeve.

As I relayed the conversation, I felt incredulous. "Too intense?" I balked. "Too intense for whom?" Against my will, tears leaked from my eyes, and I rolled my head into my free arm to wipe them away.

Maeve walked to the foot of the table. She crossed her arms and calmly stated, "People who are unkind to people in chemo are going to hell. Straight to hell." Her mouth was set in a straight line of displeasure, her nostrils flared; she was so vicariously outraged, I burst out laughing.

"Oh, I mean it," Maeve said, gravely.

"I know you do," I said. "I just love it when people seriously say things like that."

She cocked her head, "Things like what?"

"Like, 'so and so is dead to me,' and 'so and so is going to hell'—"

"Aren't those always serious statements?" she asked.

"Yes," I assured her. "They're just so wonderfully dramatic."

"Wonderfully dramatic," she said, mimicking me with the trace of a bad British accent.

"Don't," I said.

"Wonderfully dramatic," she said again, this time with rolling hand gestures.

I flung an arm over my eyes, "Stop."

She sighed. "I love the way you talk."

I lowered my arm, and instantly regretted it. I was blushing.

"'Love the way you talk,'" she repeated. "Is that grammatically correct? It sounds strange . . . "

I tried to think, stared at the ceiling; its pock marks, its water stains, its accidents. "I think that's correct," I said.

Before my diagnosis, I was never so aware of how slippery emotions were. Now, I marveled at the fact that in the course of a day, I could feel such a spectrum of feel-ings—from grief to euphoria—and still somehow manage to call my days either "good" or "bad."

Sitting across from one another, sipping Earl Greys, The Fan laughed as I told her stories about the performance art I had witnessed in graduate school.

"I shuddered," I said, concluding one tale about a naked woman and hardboiled eggs. "I absolutely shuddered."

"I think that's the whole point of performance art," The Fan said. "To make us have some sort of visceral reaction."

I smiled at her use of the word "visceral." Sometimes it seemed difficult to meet people who were eloquent, nat-urally articulate. In Milwaukee, I rarely met anyone who had a context for performance art. Rarer still, in this town where the baseball team's mascot was a giant sausage, where a freakish bronze statue of The Fonz was un-iron-ically erected along the riverfront, was locating someone who could truly grasp the meaning of "absurd."

When The Fan got up to use the bathroom, I consid-ered all that I was omitting from our conversation—the surgeries, the cancer, the chemo, the radiation that had concluded three weeks prior. She, on the other hand, had told me about her two kids, about her divorce—a divorce that had left her a rather wealthy woman (hence the new Audi)—about her love affair with Milwaukee, about how she spent her weeks and weekends: hiking, farmers' mar-kets, road trips, book clubs...

I ran a hand back and forth over my head, still shocked to feel hair there. I looked around the coffee house at the other patrons. Some were alone, some in small groups, some in pairs. I felt a pang of longing, *If only I was in Chicago* ...

In the corner was a loud group of men and women. The coffee house served alcohol, and it was apparent this group had had too much of it.

"Maybe I'll date a military chick," said one of the men. I knew he was referring to me. My shoulders tightened; I wanted to break his nose, and while he bled, hold his head up by the hair, look him in his blackening eyes and say, "Chemo, motherfucker. Chemo."

Instead, I shot him a dirty look—and though drunk, his expression suggested he registered my warning, and the table quieted. The Fan returned from the restroom.

"You know what I was thinking?" she beamed.

"What?"

"I should be your official Milwaukee tour guide."

Frankly, I could think of little worse—chemo, maybe— than having some woman, this woman, drag me around Milwaukee in her expensive car, trying to persuade me to share her enthusiasm. I laughed politely, sipped my tea. "Okay."

"Seriously," she said, lowering her voice, as a smirk tipped across her face. "I could make Milwaukee very interesting."

"Okay," Maeve said during one of our last sessions. "Now's your chance: ask me anything you need to know."

I smiled weakly. I wanted to know lots of things, none related to the loss of my lymph nodes. I felt I'd earned a Master's degree in breast cancer and breast cancer surgery aftermath. I wanted to know more about Maeve. What music did she like? Which authors? I knew she kept a little notebook where she sometimes jotted down titles of books she wanted to read. Did she drink? Had she ever smoked pot? How did she meet her husband? Incidentally, I knew she liked AC/DC and, at weddings, enjoyed dancing more than her husband did. I knew her children's ages and that one played football while another was in the early stages of relinquishing her Barbie dolls. I knew she was originally from the suburbs of Chicago, like me. I knew she loved Golden Retrievers and Milwaukee's lakeshore. What else? I had a million questions.

I shrugged. "Is there anything I can do to avoid getting 'big arm'?"

"Big arm" was a crude term for lymphedema, a chronic swelling of the arm brought on by lymph node removal. I used to joke about it with Emily, *I'm gonna be a tit-less dyke with one gigantic arm.*

Maeve suggested I visit a medical supply company to purchase a sleeve that would assuage "big arm" should it ever become an issue.

"All right," I said.

"Do you know where the medical supply company is?"

"Oh, yes," I said. "Whenever I move to a new city, I make sure to find out where the grocery store is, where the post office is, where the library is, and where the medical supply company—"

"Stop," she said, laughing. "Mequon. It's in Mequon."

Though I had no concept of where Mequon was, I nodded.

"Wait," she said, "you don't have a car—"

"I'll figure something out."

She asked if I had Fridays off from work. "Because I have Fridays off," she said. "I could take you on a Friday."

I shook my head, waved my hands dismissively. "No. Absolutely not."

"Why?"

"You've helped me plenty," I said. "I can't let you use a day off—"

"She doth protest too much," Maeve said brightly, misquoting Shakespeare. "Don't you think that sounds like fun? A field trip to the medical supply company?"

"She's taking me to Mequon," I told my sister. "On her day off. How nice is that?"

"What the hell is Mequon?" my sister asked.

"Some town in Wisconsin," I replied. I just liked saying the name. The word felt like an inside joke between Maeve and myself.

When Maeve came to pick me up that warm morning in August, I was waiting on the steps outside my apartment building; bald-headed in a Pink Floyd t-shirt, torn blue jeans, and flip-flops. Chemo had made my toenails fall out and, never one to care about the appearance of my feet, that day I felt oddly self-conscious.

Maeve, too, was in blue jeans and sandals. Her toenails shone, a warm red. She wore sunglasses, principally used to push her hair from her face, and for the first time I regarded her as beautiful.

The medical supply company was a stark, beige, one-story building in an otherwise abandoned industrial park just outside Mequon "proper."

"Pretty," I said as we pulled into the parking lot.

Maeve smirked. "I told you," she said. "Just like a day at the art museum."

The woman who fitted me for my arm sleeve was in her late-sixties—stout, chatty, with dark lipstick and powder blue eye-shadow, a stiffly sprayed pageboy several months grown out. While she pinched measuring tape around my arm, she asked if I liked Harleys.

"Don't know much about them," I said.

"Oh!" she cried. "My husband and me are crazy about 'em. Some say we're too old for Hogs, but I say, 'Age ain't nothin' but a number...'"

I snuck a conspiratorial glance at Maeve as the woman continued, but Maeve's face was still and attentive as a pastor's.

While the woman rang me up for the sleeve, she fussed with her hair, then mumbled, "Bad hair day."

At this, Maeve glanced furtively in my direction, a half smile on her face.

I bit my lip and looked away, but it was Maeve who laughed first.

"Oh," the Harley enthusiast said, deeply embarrassed. "I shouldn't have said that."

"It's all right," I assured her, smiling at Maeve. "It's all relative."

Back in the car, Maeve clapped a hand on my thigh. "You, my dear, are full of tact and resilience."

"No thanks to you," I replied.

She shoved my knee. "Now what?"

I shrugged.

"Do you need to run some errands?"

I laughed, shook my head.

"Not grocery shopping?" She said. "Not a trip to Target for socks?"

"I'm afraid not."

She sighed theatrically. "Wanna go for a drive?"

"Yes," I said. "I would like that."

Maeve took me far north and then back down what I call,

to the displeasure of Milwaukeeans I know, "Milwaukee's version of Lake Shore Drive. " She pointed out the street where she lived with her husband and children. She pointed out a sculpture along the lake, a giant human figure, crouched at the water's edge.

"That's my absolute favorite," she said.

I remembered her telling me about the sculpture during one of our sessions, insisting I drive up to see it. In her description, she never mentioned that the body was comprised of letters: a tangled alphabet. The overlapping letters gave the figure a disordered appearance, a sort of gibberish in human form.

"It's beautiful," I told her.

After tea, I was done with The Fan. I told her I had to go home.

"I have a dog that needs walking," I explained.

"Oh," The Fan said. "Can I come with?"

I hesitated. "Go with . . . to walk the dog?"

By this point, any ounce of attraction I may have felt toward The Fan had evaporated. She was too insistent, a quality I was only keen on where it concerned artistic and academic affairs. But my inner-Frankenstein protested, "Friend. Good."

"Sure," I told The Fan. "But I can't let you into my apartment. It's a disaster."

"Oh, that's fine," said The Fan, cheerily. "Do you know that story where the woman tells this guy she won't let him in because her apartment is a disaster and then, like five months later, they're dating and their place is basically a hoarder house—"

I smiled tersely. "I don't know that story."

"What's the dog's name?" The Fan asked.

"Bernie," I said.

She laughed. "And he's a little wiener dog?"

"Yes," I affirmed. "A dachshund."

My last appointment with Maeve was a week after my radiation treatments began. Radiation was five days a week. Within four days, the skin on my breast and under my arm had turned pink. Maeve had prepared me for the fact that radiation would bring about the end of our sessions. She couldn't stretch me if my skin was burned. "I would hurt you," she explained.

At the start of our final meeting, Maeve asked to see my skin. Modestly, I rolled up the sleeve of my T-shirt, allowing her a glimpse of the ruddy flesh near my armpit. She frowned, shook her head. "That doesn't tell me anything."

I blinked at her.

"Off with the shirt."

My mouth fell open.

There were days when it felt like the janitor was the only person at the cancer center who hadn't seen and manipulated my breast, days when I removed my shirt so many times the act felt as routine as brushing my teeth.

"My whole shirt?" I stammered.

"Well," she said, "enough that I can see."

Raising my arms, I felt my face flush and had to gulp down a sob. Maeve and I were close now; she wasn't supposed to see.

The Fan talked incessantly as Bernie and I walked from my apartment back to her car. She talked about music, the nineties, San Diego, Indian food. She talked about coffee shops she liked and nail polish she had purchased. She talked about walking.

When we arrived at her car, we exchanged cell phone numbers and she said, "Are you sure you're done for the night?"

"Yeah," I yawned, affectedly. "I'm pretty beat."

"Okay," she said, glancing down at her shoes. "But I must admit I'm a little disappointed. I was kind of expecting more."

Though I believe "guffaw" is an expression reserved for Batman comics, I guffawed. "Sorry to disappoint."

"No worries," she said. "I'll text you later."

I'm sure you will, I thought. *Repeatedly*.

But as soon as Bernie and I had walked away, I wanted to text The Fan. I thought of Emily, *That woman was totally coming on to you*.

I could have gone home with The Fan. I could have taken her home, and when we were panting on the couch, half-naked and sweaty, I could have said: "So, one of my breasts has no nipple and I have a bunch of red radiation tattoos on my sternum and torso and you need to be gentle with my left arm because I don't want to get lymphedema. See, I forgot to tell you that I had cancer, which is the real reason I've done nothing since I've lived in this nightmare hellhole. Now, let's get it on." My hook-up days, at least the easy ones, were over.

On a quiet side street, I kicked a tree and blamed the aggression on estrogen blocker-triggered mood swings. Further down, I kicked another tree for having estrogen blockers to blame my mood swings on.

At home, with Bernie, I did as I'd planned. I brushed

my teeth. I took my estrogen blocker. I donned my pajamas—an old Jane's Addiction concert T-shirt and boxer shorts. Sometimes, I would tell Maeve about my life before cancer. Funny stories, odd stories.

. . . So there is my uncle, chaining this burning tree to a car . . .

. . . and fully clothed, I jumped into that filthy river to get the damn sunglasses . . .

. . . so there I was, at this gallery in the South Loop, drunk on whiskey and quoting T. S. Eliot . . .

She laughed at my stories, and her laughter gave credence to the life I lived before. I imagined telling her about my night with The Fan.

And so she says, "Can I go with to walk your dog?"

I could hear her laughter, her retort, something about being "too compromising," something about "being nice." And I could imagine suppressing a wry smile, rolling my eyes at her plain-gorgeous face, and saying, "I'm tired of being nice."

Two years later, on my way to work, standing in line at Starbucks, waiting an inordinate amount of time on an iced coffee, I heard someone other than the barista call my name. Still as bereft of a social life as I had been my first year in Milwaukee, I figured I was being summoned by a student or co-worker. Since moving out of Milwaukee proper and into the neighboring suburb of Shorewood, I tended to run into these types more often—at the grocery store, while walking the dog, at Starbucks.

I turned to see Maeve.

"What are you doing this far north?" she squealed, moving in to hug me.

"I live here," I said. "I mean, down the road. Not here, per se, though it sometimes feels like I live here, at Starbucks," I stammered like a girl with a crush.

Maeve laughed. "So life's treating you well these days! You live near, but not in, a Starbucks."

I nodded.

She introduced me to her daughter, a girl with a headful of curls and a mouthful of braces, saying, "This is my friend, Allison."

I appreciated that. I appreciated that she didn't introduce me as her "former patient" in front of strangers waiting on iced lattes and caramel macchiatos. While her daughter knew what she did for a living, my fellow Starbucks customers did not, and that morning I was looking a bit harried: "psychiatric," onlookers would have concluded.

We made vague plans to walk our dogs together, but we didn't exchange email addresses or phone numbers. I scurried out of Starbucks ahead of Maeve and her daughter. I was running late for work and couldn't stay. I boarded the bus knowing we'd probably never see each other again, but still, I was happy.

I never knew how to define Maeve, but there, introducing me to her kid, she gave me a word I could comprehend: "friend."

Good.

ACKNOWLEDGEMENTS

First and foremost, I would like to express my sincerest gratitude to George Braziller, for publishing this collection. I am honored.

For working tirelessly to find a home for these essays, and for seeing me through my anxieties about the process, I am forever in debt to my intrepid agent and friend, Cicily Janus.

I feel remarkably fortunate to have been paired with such an incredibly gifted editor, Lexi Freiman. Thank you for believing in this work, for your vision, brilliance, and good humor. I feel we've been on an amazing journey together – and indeed, we have.

For supporting me, putting up with me, and loving me, I must also thank my parents, Dennis and Joanne. Don't think for a moment that I don't know, and deeply appreciate, all that you've done for me. I love you both very much.

In my life, I have been undeservedly blessed with family members and countless friends who have loved me, taken care of me, encouraged me, spoke truth to me, saw me through some hard times, listened to my stories, and made me laugh. I simply would not have the courage to write without those of you who have stood by me through the years, especially, Kristine O'Sullivan, Joanne Blumenshine, Heather Gruber, Hope Radtke, Marilynne Babiak, Megan Johnston-Spencer, Shirley Goldyn, Randi Frank, Miriam Pollack, Judy Hoffman, Lynn Loewen, Angie Gruber, Jeremy Hooper, Jessica Pedersen, Christopher Gruber, Cheryl Coan, Joe Babiak, Dana Vinger, and countless others I haven't the space to name. You all make me so happy. You all inspire me. Without you, life just wouldn't be worth writing about.

Lastly, I owe an enormous debt of gratitude to the gifted medical professionals who cared for me during my most difficult year – particularly Dr. Alexandra Lal, Dr. Varsha Shah, Molly Megan, Deb Theine, and every single nurse in Columbia St. Mary's cancer center. They saw me through profound hardship with astonishing kindness and compassion, and I will never forget that. My sincerest, most heartfelt thanks to each of you for giving me a bit more time on this mortal coil, and for doing so with humor and grace.

ALLISON GRUBER

Allison Gruber's prose has appeared in a number of literary journals, and in the anthology *Windy City Queer: Dispatches from the Third Coast*. She has been a poet-in-residence with The Poetry Center of Chicago. She holds an MFA in Writing from the School of the Art Institute of Chicago, and lives with her partner in Flagstaff, Arizona.